What oth

"Very well set out easy to understand course... This book takes the reader through a series of purposeful exercises to increase concentration, focus, and awareness."
Tami Brady, editor, Canada

"This guide gave me what other websites and books about astral travel did not. It gave me down-to-earth, practical and very effective techniques to explore astral travel and lucid dreaming. Through allowing me to get experiences, it also showed me that there is so much more there is to life than what we can experience through our five senses; so much information and potential that can really enhance your existence...Highly recommended to anyone who wants practical techniques rather than lots of theory."
David Gardner, freelance designer, Australia

"If you are looking for something that will totally open your eyes to experiencing the multi-dimensionality of life, Astral Projection is what you need. And to learn to do it, this book is a must! If you want to project, all you have to do is follow the author's directions to the t. It's as simple as that!"
Michael Sinclair, United States

"This book is very different from any of the other books I have looked at. It leaves the theory at a minimum and cuts straight to the chase, which is how to actually experience the astral plane!...Using the techniques in this book and practicing in a disciplined way, in only three or so years I have been able to have literally hundreds of out of body experiences, and experience the astral on a very regular basis, whereas before I came across this information I had never experienced anything like that in my entire life."
Andrew Puls, United States

A Course in
ASTRAL TRAVEL
and DREAMS

by Belzebuub

ABSOLUTE
PUBLISHING GROUP

First edition, September 2004, cloth (ISBN: 0-9740560-1-4)

Absolute Publishing Group LLC
P.O. Box 99167, Emeryville, CA 94662, U.S.A
www.absolutepublishinggroup.com

Book and cover design by Patricia Atkinson
Illustrations by Angela McIlveen and Camilla Mullins

Printed and bound in the United States of America on acid-free paper and soy based inks.

ISBN-10:   0-9740560-3-0
ISBN-13:   978-0-9740560-3-6

Library of Congress Control Number: 2005929522

IMPORTANT NOTICE

This publication is intended to provide helpful and informative material on the subjects addressed herein and is purchased with the understanding that the author and publisher are not engaged in rendering professional advice or services to the individual reader.

The information contained in this book is not intended as a substitute for consulting with a health care professional. If you are suffering any medical condition, we encourage you to consult with a medical professional.

The accuracy and completeness of the information provided herein and the advice stated herein is not guaranteed or warranted to produce any particular results and the advice and strategies provided may not be suitable for every individual.

The author and the publisher disclaim any liability for loss, injury, or damages resulting directly or indirectly from the use or application of any of the contents of this book including any loss or injury resulting directly or indirectly from the negligence of the author or publisher. Any application of the material set forth in the following pages is at the reader's discretion and is his or her sole responsibility.

CONTENTS

A Preface to the Course

*T*his is a comprehensive introductory course in Astral travel and dreams. It will take you step-by-step along the techniques and exercises that will allow you to experience Astral travel and to have out-of-body experiences. It will explain what the Astral world is and what you can do when you go there consciously. It also explains what dreams are, how you can remember them well, what their relationship with Astral travel is, what they mean, where they come from, how you can use them to understand yourself better and to improve your daily life. The course is a solid foundation to get you off to a good start in your Astral travels and forms a sound basis for further exploration.

It is run both on the Internet and in study centers where it is taught to live groups. It has been very successful in terms of getting people to actually experience the Astral plane, so its contents are very much already tried and tested.

As well as reading the material here, you should participate week by week in the free course online at the Gnosticweb website *www.gnosticweb.com* or in a study center, where you can get feedback to your questions as you progress along the course and can communicate with other people.

I have been teaching groups of people to Astral project since 1990 and on the Internet since 2000. So I know that the exercises given here do work. I have been gradually refining them over time, discovering why some things work and others do not.

I wasn't born with the ability to Astral project like some people, so I had to learn how to do it, sometimes with great struggle, overcoming many obstacles until the techniques succeeded. I now have a lot of experience of being out-of-the-body, not only in the Astral plane, but in other planes too.

However, I give very little of what I have experienced of the Astral plane in this course, because most of it requires further explanation. Instead, I have concentrated upon compiling a straightforward and effective set of techniques, which you can use to begin your incredible journey of self-discovery, should you wish to.

Years of hard work and experience beyond the three-dimensional world, along with years of teaching, has allowed me to gather techniques that work most effectively and to be able to pass on solutions to overcome the most common difficulties encountered.

If you are in reach of one of the study centers where this course is taught, I can recommend the group exercises that are carried out in study centers to anyone learning to Astral travel. It can be quite exciting to get together at weekends with other like-minded people and spend the whole time practicing to get into the Astral plane. It's common to find at least one person who gets out of their body at each attempt and it is great to lie down as a group and to get up and see someone else already out. The days and nights become magical. I hope that this course will bring that magic into people's lives and that it will enable many more people to explore into the multi-dimensional reality of life.

When you go to try to Astral travel, you will be more successful if you make up your mind to follow what is written in this course as a complete course rather than just read it through, or skim through bits of it at random and then practice the exercises from it here and there. That is because the different exercises and techniques all follow on from one another. So for getting the best results they should be practiced in the order and in the nine-week timeframe that I give in the course.

This timeframe will give you enough time to experience something of the Astral plane; the more dedicated and disciplined you are towards it, the more likely you are to have success.

This course is not about experiencing all aspects of the Astral plane and the esoteric worlds - it is about learning and exploring the techniques for Astral travel. It will enable you to get there and will give you most of what you need to travel out-of-the-body. But to really explore that plane fully you need much more information than this course can provide. For this reason I run other courses, which explain in more depth what is going on in the Astral world and in the human psyche. You will really need these other courses if you want to explore the Astral plane fully, because there is so much going on there that the courses will help you to know about.

Anyone can learn to project, but it is quite another thing to know how to make best use of time spent in the Astral plane. For that you have to know about the secret esoteric world and what the human psyche consists of. Then you will really use your Astral journeys fruitfully and will have the chance to become a competent esotericist. Without this knowledge, you will only be able to gain incipient, basic information and will be trying to make sense of the unknown without the ability to do so.

I realize that some of the information towards the end of the course, such as that contained in the dream symbols and the conjuration's will sound strange to many people who are not familiar with this field of study, but I have had to mention these more esoteric kinds of information for the sake of completeness of the course and their importance in the study of the Astral plane. It is also worth bearing in mind that this course is part of a series of courses, where esoteric things are explained in more detail in the later Journey to Enlightenment course. So I recommend that if there is something that you don't understand here, rather than being put off by it, continue with future courses so that you go deeper in the study. In the Astral plane, many things are obscure at first because our values are taken primarily from the three-dimensional world when we begin the search of higher dimensions and the exploration into the nature of reality. But like learning to make sense of this world as we grow up, the Astral plane and the higher dimensions do make more sense with experience and with a reliable teaching as a guide.

This course will be a valuable tool to get started and to learn to experience the Astral world. If you practice the exercises properly, you will discover a lot about life and it will amaze you, but when you do, you will also find that you have a whole lot more to discover. We are alive in the three-dimensional world for just a short time, but we exist in eternity; it is there to be explored.

The Topics on the Course

There are nine weekly topics in all, and each contains reading material. There is an additional exercise every week for you to try at home each day and, once enough has been learned, there is a group exercise that you can follow online or in a study center, where everyone on the courses throughout the world tries to get to the same place at the same time.

This is one of a series of four courses. The others are: *Searching Within*, which studies the inner life of thoughts, emotions, relationships and change; the *Journey to Enlightenment* course, which explains more about what the overall scheme of things is and continues to develop the Astral exercises; and the *Advanced Investigation* course, which allows a time to concentrate solely upon the exercises and to develop the skill levels in them to a higher degree. The overall aim of the whole series of courses is to give the effective techniques for personal exploration and transformation, to explain what's really going on in life and to show how to walk the path of spiritual and inner awakening.

Here is a list of the topics:

Week 1 - An Introduction to Astral Travel and Dreams
Week 2 - Preparing for Astral Projection
Week 3 - The Process of Astral Projection
Week 4 - The Influence of the Psyche
Week 5 - Waking Up in the Astral Plane from Dreams
Week 6 - Mantras for Astral Projection
Week 7 - Dealing With Negative Entities
Week 8 - Astral and Dream Experiences
Week 9 - Where to Go From Here

Each weekly topic is followed by a weekly exercise.

Weekly Exercises on the Course

The weekly exercises follow a sequence starting with techniques to remember dreams and relaxation, moving on to exercises to prepare for Astral projection, techniques to project and to get consciously into the Astral plane from a dream, then leading into learning to explore in the Astral plane and finally to a group exercise to meet up in one place.

The general types of techniques taught on the course to achieve an Astral experience are:

1. Astral projection:
   a) Concentration/visualization (this can cover a large number of different exercises)
   b) Mantras

2. Waking up in the Astral plane while being in a dream:
   a) Questioning and recording triggers
   b) Increasing the level of awareness in daily life

Building Skills and Developing Abilities

The course provides not just an explanation of techniques, but it also shows how to build up the initial skills needed for Astral projection. The skills are taught from the beginning of the course and are used to explore things in the Astral plane later in the course. The explorations are designed to make use of the techniques of Astral projection as a means of effectively exploring the Astral plane and discovering the truth of things.

The period of building skills is similar to acquiring skills for almost anything. An athlete needs to train in order to race for example, or a builder needs to learn a whole range of things in order to build a building. Rushing into a technique is ineffective. It's like an athlete running a race without training. For an athlete the training develops technique, physical endurance, strength, etc.

Although Astral experiences can happen suddenly and without any preparation whatsoever, preparation is required for most people to achieve them on a regular basis. With the preparation then it's possible to have Astral experiences regularly.

An important aim of the course is to learn how to be a competent investigator of the Astral plane. This will help to ensure that the out-of-body experiences of other people are not held as unprovable beliefs, or that fear does not prevent personal investigation and the search for the truth, as it is better to learn to use and trust your own abilities. By not trusting your own abilities there is a tendency to rely upon others, upon second-hand information and that is where many problems and much confusion begins.

It's important to be able to learn and apply the most effective techniques you possibly can, in order to find out the truth of things. By doing the exercises on the course you will learn to develop your own Astral abilities and to trust them and discover information for yourself. This is much better than running from one book or web site to another looking for intellectual answers as some do.

This is an intensive course so you need to do the exercises as best as you can in the order you get them if you want them to work most effectively. If you mix these exercises up with techniques from elsewhere while you are doing this course, you may find the exercises here less effective. That is because they require continuity and single mindedness, rather than a superficial attempt, and because other techniques may have the effect of watering these ones down. It's worth dedicating the time the course takes to doing it properly and thoroughly.

Belzebuub

Week 1

AN INTRODUCTION TO ASTRAL TRAVEL AND DREAMS

*W*e are all familiar in a way with the Astral plane although we may not realize it. That's because it's the place that we go to in dreams. But what we call Astral travel is being in that place while consciously being aware of it, just as we are aware of being here in this three-dimensional world. These kinds of experiences are also called out-of-body experiences and they may happen while dreaming or while consciously leaving the physical body; sometimes spontaneously, sometimes induced, or sometimes in situations such as near death experiences

Although Astral experiences are fairly common (a fair sized percentage of people have had at least one), they are all too often not understood - not by the person who has had one, nor by friends, family, doctors, scientists, etc, although they are a real and very natural part of life. Even though many people

1

will not have had conscious Astral experiences, everyone has had dreams, and they are part of the Astral world. We all go to the Astral plane every night when we go to sleep. This course will help you to get there consciously and will show you how to explore it; you could also learn many things about yourself too.

The Astral Plane

The Astral plane is one of two planes that constitute the fifth dimension. Science in quantum physics postulates the likelihood of parallel universes existing and includes the fifth dimension in this, due to the discovery that minute particles behave unpredictably according to laws different to ours. They are correct in this since the laws of the fifth dimension are different and it is at this molecular level that the physical and the fifth dimensions meet.

Going to that dimension is, however, an internal science. To do it you have to explore it from within your own psyche and that is where contemporary science effectively leaves it. This however, is where we begin, because this is an internal science, which involves study, experimentation, experience and the gaining of knowledge.

There are four main ways to have an out-of-body experience in the Astral plane. The first is to project, the second is to wake up in a dream (to know that you are in one and to realize that it's the Astral), the third is to have a near death experience and the fourth is with death.

Being in the Astral is provable to those who do it, although there have been many cases of people seeing objects, places or events while out of the body, then later being able to tell others about them, while to observers they were asleep and had no way of knowing about them. It is something real; it is not a figment of the imagination, but another place that exists.

As I mentioned earlier, we are all familiar in a way with the Astral because it's the place that we go to in dreams. However, in an Astral experience you are actually there and you can know that you are there, in the same way that you know that you are in the physical world.

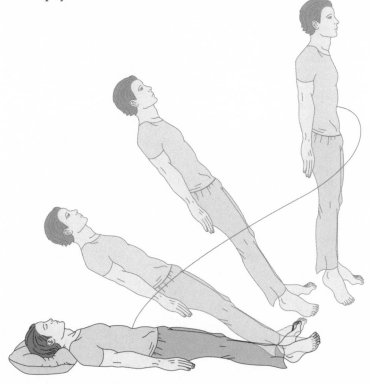

The Astral is governed by its own laws. So you are able to fly; you can jump into the air and fly upwards, looking down over your house and the area where you live. It will look very often as it does normally. Then, as many people have done, you can fly somewhere.

It is more exciting than anything you can read in a book or watch at the cinema; it is something that really happens to you. You actually find yourself in another dimension, existing outside the physical world. You will be able to fly, go through walls and objects, meet people, travel to distant places in the world and beyond - it is a profound experience.

Visiting the Astral plane can change your whole view of life. You can travel and have a bit of experience here and there but it's a huge waste to treat it superficially or like a hobby. It's far better to have the aim to do something fundamentally worthwhile, which is to discover what is really going on in this life and to receive spiritual knowledge and to walk the path to enlightenment.

With this in mind, in the Astral you can meet and receive teachings from spiritual beings - those who have founded or have been mentioned in the world's great religions, in mythology or in esotericism. You can discover secret knowledge, learn about yourself and see where your spiritual obstacles and your inner defects are. You can monitor your spiritual progress and can walk along the spiritual path knowing each step that you have made, learn hidden wisdom about death, the process of awakening, get premonitions of the future, receive guidance, discover the purpose of life, discover what happens with death and much more.

Just by being in the Astral you can get access to incredible knowledge that is denied the majority of people in the world who do not go there consciously. However, you can get much more if you walk along the spiritual path, receiving knowledge and experience beyond what you can imagine.

You will get more out of it if you consider the Astral not just in terms of going to another dimension, but in terms of what you can do there and what are the best and most effective things you can do while you are there. After all, time in that dimension, consciously that is, is limited compared to the time spent in the physical world, so it makes sense to make good use of it.

Not surprisingly, you can learn a lot about death from the Astral, because the dead go into the other dimensions. Visions, divine visitations, spiritual beings of all kinds, apparitions in religions and mythology, all have their root in the higher dimensions.

Beings both spiritual and negative exist in the fifth dimension and if you travel enough you will meet both kinds. To explain why they are there, how they got there and what they are doing is something that is explained in a later course. This course will, if you practice, allow you to see something of what is going on beyond the physical world and will give techniques to objectively explore the Astral plane. It's really important to find out what's going on. I could tell you of what I know now, but that would become something to either accept or reject, so it's better to give the techniques so that you can actually go and find out for yourself - if you want to that is.

If you try this Astral course superficially or on its own and just leave it at that without going on to the other courses, you are likely try to explore the Astral a little like a hallucinating person, seeing what are mostly the projections of your own subconscious, because the subconscious must be tackled for objective Astral experiences. Also the information on the Journey to Enlightenment course gives an overall picture of what's going on and gives the techniques for serious investigation.

My First Astral Projection

It is possible to meet different people in the Astral plane, as you will see from looking at the group exercises on the courses.

But I'll say a little about my first projection, which was the first Astral experience I had.

I was with a group of about twelve people doing a practice in a Gnostic Center. It was night-time and the instructor asked us to go into a special practice room and to look at everything in it very intensively. I observed everything in the room in great detail; the ceiling, the walls, all the objects. We were in silence and I tried to look as clearly as possible without thoughts clouding my perception. As one of the others came into the room I could see him, even though I had my back to him. I almost said "Hello Dave" without turning around to face him, but I couldn't because we had to be silent. When we felt really 'there', each of us went back into the other room, to lie down and to try to project back into the room we had just observed. The instructor had told us that he was going to place an object in that room while we were lying down and he had given us the task to go back there in the Astral and to see what was put in it.

As I lay down I tried to keep that awareness, not letting myself be taken away with thoughts. I concentrated on the room intensively, remembering all the little details that I had seen. Soon afterwards I began to rise out of my body; everything seemed strange. It was such a new and shocking feeling that I became very frightened and shouted "Help, help." But no one could hear me physically because I was in the Astral plane. I looked around and saw that the instructor had also projected. He was sitting there and another man had appeared in the room. He had been drawn into the room by the strength of the exercise. My fear unfortunately brought me back to my body. I looked around and I was surprised that no one had heard me shouting.

Later on I spoke to the instructor and he confirmed that the gentleman who we both knew had been there. Although it was brief, it was an amazing experience; I had discovered that it was possible to leave the physical body and even to meet with people there.

Now I'll say a little about dreams and their relationship to the Astral plane.

Dreams

Every night with sleep, dreams occur, whether they are remembered or not. In dreams what usually happens is that the images from the subconscious become real for the dreamer, and they exist in the world that has been projected from the subconscious. Not all dreams are projections of the subconscious however; some are events actually taking place in the Astral plane, while others are scenes or places that are put there by ones own Being or by awakened Beings (Masters) for the purpose of teaching.

With sleep, we leave behind the physical body, which holds the psyche onto the physical plane. We leave behind the sensory impressions of the three dimensional world and enter the fifth dimension - what we call the Astral plane. We are connected then to the physical body through a silver cord, which makes it impossible to not come back to the body after we have woken up. So, while we dream messages are sent from us, the psyche, in the Astral, to our physical body, including the brain and vice versa, through that silver cord. Although it is there, the silver cord is not normally seen when Astral traveling.

Now, being without a physical body, there is no physical world to see, touch and taste; so what is left are thoughts, emotions and consciousness - but you are in the Astral plane. Unfortunately, when there (either when dreaming or when traveling consciously) what is actually in the Astral plane is not normally seen, or it is only seen partially because of the images of the mind, which are projected onto it. Even if what is seen there is real it is common not to even realize or question that you are there. It is the nature of that plane that one creates ones own world, which is not real. But there is something real there, only it is not normally seen when dreaming or is only partially seen through the haze of projected images. To see what is there, we must be aware (which I will explain more about in future classes) and be clear of the images projected by the subconscious.

When in the dreams, the process of daydreaming that occurred during the day continues. Dreams occur at night because of the daydream of thoughts, images and emotions of the subconscious (the egos, or selves) that take place during the day. Going through the day like that one is rarely aware of the information of the five senses - of the reality of where you are at any given moment. Therefore, when sleep arrives there is also a lack of awareness of where one is.

Sometimes when dreaming you do actually see what is there in the Astral. It is because there can sometimes be periods of lucidity. In these periods someone may see what really exists in the Astral world or dream about a place that actually exists in the physical world (even though they may never have seen it and discover it later physically). In these clear times it is possible to learn quite a lot; higher beings can show you things or teach you and they can awaken the consciousness, clearing the projections of the subconscious in order to teach something. You could also as another example have a premonition about something that will happen in the future, something which you could have had no way of knowing - yet you see the event in a dream and it comes true.

Sometimes the dreams themselves can have a symbolic meaning. So it's worth paying close attention to what you see either in dreams or when consciously in the Astral because there may be important information, possibly in the form of a symbol, a number, an event or words that are spoken. Symbols are used

8

because they are a universal language. Common symbols can be found throughout the great religions of the world. Information is often given there symbolically and the meaning of the scene or of the symbols shown in the dream can be intuitively comprehended, so its very helpful to use intuition and to learn about the spiritual path and its symbolism. Then you will be in a better position to decipher the correct meaning. You can learn to develop intuition on these courses.

Lucidity in a dream can be so great at times that you actually realize that you are dreaming and realize that you are in the Astral plane. You can be conscious in the Astral in this way as effectively as if you had projected there. This kind of experience is generally referred to as a lucid dream, but it's more accurate to say that you wake up out of a dream into the conscious experience of the Astral plane. There is a whole topic on this type of experience on this course, so I won't go into it in any more detail at this stage.

There is another type of dream, which is the nightmare. These occur when the dreamer goes to the infra-dimensions instead of the usual Astral plane. These types of dreams require quite a lot more explanation so I will leave it for another time.

There is valuable information to be gained by studying dreams, from both the meaningful ones and the ones created by the images and false scenarios projected by the subconscious. In this latter type, you may see yourself perhaps angry, fighting or stealing. They could be things that you wouldn't usually do in everyday life, or they could be things that you do usually do in everyday life. In either case, bizarre though they sometimes may be, they are an accurate reflection of what goes on in the psyche, in the conscious and subconscious processes during the day, during any day of one's life.

In the Searching Within course you learn to see these different psychological states (egos) during daily life and learn how to study dreams to get information about the states that occur during the day; for example, fear, anger or anxiety. On the Journey to Enlightenment course you learn how to get rid of the different elements of the subconscious (egos) and to replace them with consciousness. Gradually the subconscious decreases and one is more and more conscious at each moment during both dreams and daily life.

The less time spent in these subconscious states in daily life and the less we have them, the more the psyche increases in its consciousness and lucidity and, as a consequence, increases the lucidity of dreams, because they are directly related. In other words, the more aware we are in daily life, the more aware we are in dreams. Eventually then we will see the Astral exactly as it is. But that is really a part of a long process, which I will explain more about as the different courses progress.

I am going to now explain where you are going to be when you go to the Astral plane either consciously or in dreams, in relation to this three-dimensional world and to other dimensions. The outline of the different dimensions is like a map is to travelers here in the physical world; you will find it useful to have it as a reference so that you can see where things fit in.

The Different Dimensions

The Astral is the first of two planes of the fifth dimension; it is a complete dimension of life, waiting to be explored. It is the place where dreams occur, where mystical teachings are given and where the deceased go. It is possible to go there consciously, leaving the physical body behind in the three-dimensional world; this course will teach you how. It is something real. It is not a figment of the imagination, but another place that exists, and with the techniques on this course you can prove it.

There are seven dimensions in total. Most people know what the first three are (length, width and height) and the fourth, which is time, is known to science.

The fifth dimension is eternity, which is beyond time. There are two planes in that dimension: the Astral and the Mental.

The sixth dimension is the electronic world. It also has two planes: the Causal and the Buddhic.

The seventh dimension is the dimension of the Spirit.

Beyond these dimensions is the Absolute, from which the dimensions and all of life are created. There are Beings (Seraphim) known as Fire Beings that manifest the Absolute into the dimensions.

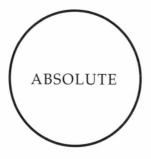

ABSOLUTE

7th - The dimension of the Spirit

6th - Electronic (2 planes) {Buddhic / Causal

5th - Eternity (2 planes) {Mental / Astral

4th - Time

3rd - Length, width and height

Infra-dimensions

The infra-dimensions are inferior zones where most people have gone to when having nightmares. They are accessible through an opening, a portal in space in the Astral plane, known in mythology as 'the mouth of Hell'. They are what are referred to as Hells in the various religions, or the Abyss.

These dimensions interpenetrate each other without mixing up; all of them are in the here and now. Certain psychic abilities can be developed to see into different dimensions from the physical plane, but all of them above the third dimension can be explored using different techniques. This course only deals with the Astral plane of the fifth dimension; it is the easiest to get to. The Journey to Enlightenment course shows how to go to planes and dimensions above that. The Absolute can be visited (not exclusively) with a transmutation technique, which is part of Alchemy, which is also on that course. The infra-dimensions can be accessed from the inferior Astral plane, where most people go to dream.

Scientific Proof for Astral Travel

It would be comforting to many starting out in Astral travel to have some kind of verification from the scientific establishment that it is real and perfectly alright to do. But you can't get that kind of absolute verification. When it comes to Astral travel you are only able to begin to talk on level terms with those who have actually done it.

There have been many experiments carried out by scientists to verify whether the Astral plane is real or whether it is a figment of the imagination. While there have been many experiments done that show the scientists that something unexplainable happens, none provide conventional science with the kind of proof that most are looking for, which will give it universal acceptance.

This is because of the methods they use to verify whether something is real or not. Their methods generally require that the scientist gets the evidence from phenomena that are external to the scientist and that the evidence is verifiable by others.

This poses problems for the scientist when it comes to Astral travel as the subject (the traveler) is in another dimension. The subject may go to a place in the Astral plane but the scientist has no evidence from the three-dimensional world that they have actually traveled anywhere. All the scientist could see was that the subject slept. Even if more than one person in the experiment meets in a place in the Astral plane, the scientist only has two or more accounts of traveling and no actual physical evidence apart from sleeping people.

This is why I refer to Astral travel as an inner science. It is only verifiable to the person who actually does it. There has been enough information given from subjects in scientific tests to show, in a common sense way at least, that Astral travel does actually happen, by accounts of traveling, seeing distant objects, places and events that actually exist, while the physical body was asleep. Yet many often absurd theories are thought of by scientists to explain what the subjects who travel to distant places out of their bodies are actually experiencing. Just as there are silly theories to explain the other kind of out-of-body experiences – near death experiences. An example of this is a person who saw what was happening on the roof of the hospital while their physical body died and, once they were revived, gave the doctors an accurate account of what was on the hospital roof. According to some scientists these kinds of experiences occur because of the death of the brain cells.

Enough attempts have been made by people trying to prove that they can travel out of their bodies to show that it is futile to try to get widespread scientific acceptance for it, no matter how compelling the account of the experience of the traveler.

It remains for the individual to prove it for themselves. I have been asked to prove that the Astral plane is real to people by traveling to their homes and telling them what's there, etc. I always declined these invitations as I would have put myself in the same situation as the subject is to the scientist in the experiment. Also because Astral traveling takes efforts and any student worth helping must learn to make their own.

Now I'll explain about some things to bear in mind when learning about dreams and exploring the Astral plane and out-of-body experiences.

The Need for Objectivity

One of the great problems with the accuracy of Astral and dream experiences is the influence of the subconscious. I will be explaining more about this on the Searching Within and Journey to Enlightenment courses, as it's beyond the scope of this course to deal with it in depth. I will mention a little about the process of the influence of the subconscious on this course, but I will explain how the psyche can become more objective and hence the out-of-body experiences more objective, in great detail in other courses.

It is very important to get this right because it is easy to be misled by the projections of the mind and to be lost in things that you read or hear from others, which are no more than projections of their subconscious and their imagination.

Any serious Astral investigator needs to be working to clear the subconscious states in a permanent way. If you 'create your own experience' while you are there, or are unconsciously influenced by your subconscious, you will miss the truth, and it is the truth that is important.

The Astral world itself, when it is not clouded by the projections of the mind, can look similar to the physical world. There you can see things that are here, as they are here. The things that are in the physical world are also in the Astral plane. So, projecting into your bedroom at night you can see it as it is in the physical world. You can get up, walk out of your room and go outside. You can see the place, the town or city where you live, the outside of your house, the street, etc, all as they are in the physical world.

Things do not always look the same though. Something may be different in your bedroom, you may project to a different place, or strange things could be going on. That's because either the mind is projecting something so you don't see it as it is, or there are actually different things there, or things have been placed there for your learning, or you have been put in a place for you to learn something.

Fear

There is another common problem when going into the Astral plane or when trying to go there and that is fear. This can be a big stoppage for many people. There are many different manifestations of that inner state. Fear of the unknown for example is very common. But you learn to overcome the fear of being in the Astral through experience, also by studying your psychology to understand and eliminate it and also by strengthening the energies of the psyche through Alchemy.

In the example of fear of the unknown, the more you do something or go somewhere and have no problems there, the less fear is associated with that place or experience. You may be afraid of eating a piece of fruit that you do not know anything about for example. However, those who know about the fruit

15

and know that its fine can eat it and even enjoy it.

Fear is what is called in modern Gnosis an ego, although many different terms have also been used such as selves, I's, psychological adjuncts, etc. By understanding and eliminating these states, in this case fear (which you will learn more about on the other courses), you gradually get rid of it.

Fear is also related to the overall state of the energies within the psyche. There is an exercise called Alchemy that transforms and strengthens the energies within the psyche. When the energies are weak there tends to be much more fear. Alchemy, which will be explained about in the Journey to Enlightenment course, strengthens the energies.

The Worry of Danger

One of the biggest fears in relation to the Astral is the fear that it is a dangerous thing to do and that it is dangerous to be there. However, it's worth bearing in mind that everyone Astral travels every night when dreaming. When you Astral project, you are aware of the whole process through which you (minus the physical body) go to the 5th dimension. When this process is new it can be very startling, and many people think that when they get into the Astral they are not going to come back. But people come back every night after dreaming. It is a normal part of life to leave the physical body behind for it to rest and recuperate its energies - we could not survive if that did not take place. It's just that with the process of Astral projection you are aware of the process that takes place when leaving the physical body and going into the Astral plane.

Another fear is that there can be entities there that will stop you from coming back or will harm you in some way. There are entities that exist in the Astral and I explain what they are and how to deal with them on this course, but they will not harm you physically in any case, so there is no need to worry about it.

Will Power for Astral Projection

Finally, if you want this course to work for you, consider that it is going to take quite a lot of effort to do it - so you have to resolve to put in that effort over the whole time of this course if you want it to succeed.

Even if you are successful in experiencing Astral travel, be prepared for the dedication, effort and work that it takes to repeat the success and to maintain it.

This is the time to set a clear goal to achieve it and to make whatever sacrifices are necessary. The more determined and single-minded you are towards achieving it the better for its success.

A conscious Astral experience can sometimes take quite a long time to achieve. So patience, effort and determination are very important; they will lay the foundation for continuity in your attempts. If it looks as though nothing is working don't give up, persist and you will eventually succeed.

Next week we'll begin to develop the skills for projection.

Questions & Answers

Below are some questions I have answered on this first topic:

Q. Is Astral travel the same as lucid dreaming?

A. Astral travel includes lucid dreaming and also travel after a conscious projection. It is being self-aware in the Astral plane of the fifth dimension, knowing you are there. Lucid dreaming is essentially the same as waking up in dreams, which is explained in a later topic on this course.

Can I move objects in the Astral environment?

You can move Astral objects in the Astral environment, just as you can move physical ones in the physical environment. The Astral plane has its own Astral matter just as the three-dimensional world does.

Is it possible to attract the attention of people in the physical world and interact with them while I move about in my Astral travels?

You are extremely unlikely to be able to interact with people who are in the physical while you are in the Astral. Although you can see the Astral part of the person who is in the physical world, whether they be shopping, etc, because of the interpenetration of the different dimensions in the here and now.

But they are different dimensions so one cannot be directly touched by the other, although they can influence each other. In the physical, three-dimensional world a person needs to have polyvision active to be able to see things from higher dimensions.

Can I move forward or back through time to any period I wish? If this is so, can I go back in time and change events, like preventing myself from making a bad decision?

You can move backwards in time in the Astral, but only through files of nature and you cannot not truly go forward either. You cannot go back in time to change events because what you see of the past are the Akashic Records. You step into what are basically records of what has happened; you cannot change past events.

Although you can see events that are going to happen while in the Astral (because events other than some accidents happen in the higher dimensions first and then move down the dimensions), it's often not 100% certain that all of the events of the future that are seen there will happen because it is possible to change circumstances here in the physical world and that alters what will eventually materialize. Usually though things don't change here and what is seen there materializes here.

Is it true that only certain people can Astral travel, and that it is the kind of thing you inherit 'genetically'?

No, anyone can learn to Astral travel. Many people who have traveled, had never done it until taught how to.

How do I ask for help from my guides when I am trying to project?

Presuming that you mean beings that have awakened for light, you call the name of the Being or angel. For example, if you call the Master Anubis, you call "Master Anubis, I invoke you" or words to that effect, over and over. You can also ask for help and guidance from your own Being. If you ever advance far enough on the Esoteric Path you can choose a Being who can help you personally.

I was wondering if taking Prozac or any other antidepressants some how affect your brain so you won't be able to Astral project?

Yes, they will affect your Astral travels, making them more difficult. They affect the consciousness which needs to be as clear as possible and the mind, which needs to be as focused as possible and the emotions which need to be absent unless they are of a superior type.

Can drugs (alcohol, marijuana, psychedelics) help you get out of your body?

They can damage your Astral body, make the mind and emotions more active and can make your consciousness more asleep, all of which are not good for continuing Astral success, not to mention the spiritual work. Cultures like the Shamans use them for experiences, but they can only go to the inferior Astral and get experiences that look spiritual sometimes, but which in fact belong to the negative side. I've seen their ceremonies in the Astral and so I know them to be negative. All drug-induced experiences belong to the negative side and that side is only strengthened in a person by taking drugs.

I just wondered if it was possible to meet with other human beings whilst Astral traveling, either while they are Astral traveling too or while they are awake and their friend has come to see them by Astral travel?

Yes, you can meet with other human beings whilst Astral traveling, but to talk to them meaningfully they also have to be conscious in the Astral. Otherwise, if you find them and they are dreaming they will often look like drunken people. They are unlikely to recognize you although they may remember seeing you in a dream. You can see people who are awake in the physical world because you see their Astral part, but you cannot communicate with them because they won't be able to see you (unless they have polyvision).

Can reduced daily eating help out-of-body experiences?

Some people say that they find OBE's easier when they eat lightly, however the main problem people have with Astral projection is that there is a lack of concentration. All you need for Astral projection is concentration and sleep, so how much you eat shouldn't have much of an affect. Having said that, it is not so good to try an Astral exercise or to go to bed after a very heavy meal because if it upsets the stomach it can take you into lower parts of the Astral. You need to be careful about eating less, fasting and so on, because it can cause other problems. As long as you are eating sensibly, I suggest you keep your regular eating pattern and continue practicing in order to improve your concentration and OBE experiences.

I really want to learn how to do this but I am scared that when I do start to split that I will become frightened and will not get to enjoy the experience.

That fear is only natural to start with, but you will overcome it as you practice. And even if you do become afraid when you split the first time, in retrospect you will cherish the experience because it is something so new and magical, and it will confirm the reality of it for you. Then after that you will be able to approach it with more stability, and it will become better and more magical if you persist.

21

Are there any moral implications to mystically uniting with a soul on the Astral plane who is married on the physical plane?

Yes, I wouldn't advise that be done. The Journey to Enlightenment course explains more about why that is.

I am very interested in gaining spiritual knowledge through Astral travel but is it also possible to gain knowledge on any other subjects while out traveling? Information we can use in the physical?

Yes, you can; the Astral plane is a source of all sorts of knowledge. But bear in mind that much is taught there through symbols too and that you are not alone when you go there.

If I Astral travel, is my body sleeping and resting so that I will wake up refreshed as always, or will it be tired after you start traveling?

Yes, if we Astral travel, the body sleeps just the same as normal. So when you wake up, you feel refreshed the same too because the Vital or Etheric body charges it up while we sleep.

After starting to travel, will you be able to return to normal sleep?

Once you start to Astral travel, you need to keep doing the exercises to keep going there, otherwise very little usually happens and the sleep goes back to normal. At the end of traveling you usually go back to your body and wake straight up in it, or the Astral turns into a dream and you wake up the next morning remembering usually that you have traveled.

What's the difference between an out-of-body experience and Astral projection?

Out-of-body experiences cover all experiences of being out of the physical body in the Astral and higher planes, while Astral projection refers specifically to projecting out of the physical body into the fifth dimension.

When you project, why can you still see things on the material plane?

When you project, you are not seeing actual physical matter but the Astral part of what is in the physical world, because everything that exists here also exists there.

Is there ever any chance I won't be able to get back to my physical body after I've been Astral traveling?

No, we are attached to the physical body by a silver cord that always brings us back. We go to the Astral every night when we go to sleep. The only difference with Astral traveling is that we are aware of the fact that we're in another dimension instead of dreaming and not being aware of it. In fact, you usually get pulled back to your body too soon; the hard part is staying out there.

Is there any chance that someone else could get into my physical body while I'm off traveling in my Astral body?

No, there is no danger of that happening. You are attached to your own physical body by the silver cord, so only you can get in. That is, unless you decide to become a medium or to channel, in which case all kinds of negative entities can get in without you knowing (not recommended).

What is the best way to get rid of an unwanted attacker while trying to leave the body?

Assuming you are talking about an Astral attacker, to deal with them properly you need to use the conjurations, which

23

are explained later on the course.

Can other beings within the Astral plane sever the silver cord?

The cord is severed by divine beings when the appointed moment of death arrives.

What is the difference between lucid dreaming and Astral projection?

The difference between lucid dreaming and Astral projection is that you project from your body during projection, while in lucid dreaming you become conscious that you are in the Astral from a dream. Sometimes though, in lucid dreaming the dream images can distort what is there. But as long as you are not affected by those you can be in the same place and do the same things as if you had projected there.

My friend who's interested in Astral travel told me that while out of the body, if there is a spirit around your body while your spirit is away, traveling, it can take over your body. Is that true?

No, a spirit can't take over your body like that.

I am just beginning to do the exercises and looking forward to Astral travel (hopefully). I'm curious whether I can go to a place that I want to in the real world when I Astral travel. Say if I want to go to an exact place at an exact time, is it possible?

You can travel to any place in the physical world but you will see its Astral part, not the physical one, because you are in a different dimension and see the things that are there. The dimensions intermingle and everything that is in the physical has an Astral part. We have an exercise at the end of the course where students meet up in a place, so you can try that if you want to precisely find out.

I have read and heard lots of rumors about things you can do while Astral traveling e.g. go back and forward in time. So I was wondering, would you be able to come into contact with departed relatives or loved ones through Astral travel? Any information on this subject would be appreciated.

You can go back in time, because it has already happened and everything is recorded in Akashic files. The future is different; events permeate down the different dimensions until they reach here.

So we can see or be in things that have yet to happen. Sometimes though our actions here can change the events that were going to happen.

You can come into contact with departed relatives or loved ones through Astral travel, because a recently deceased person is in the other dimensions. But you mostly see their personality, which is what would usually be the part most recognizable as the person. You can talk to them and they recognize you.

As my family lives far away, say for example I get the feeling that my sister is unhappy or in trouble and I want to check on her. If I become adept at Astral travel, can I travel in my Astral body to where she is located in her physical body, unaware of me, and check that she is alright? In other words, can the Astral body travel through the physical world and, although it is obviously removed from the physical, still view the physical plane as it exists in physical reality? Or is everything you would experience in the Astral body necessarily 'false', i.e. if I told myself I wanted to go see my sister and suddenly I was there next

to her, asleep or whatever, is that my real sister in her real bedroom at home in the real world or is it just a dream 'vision' of my sister?

I'm just wondering because sometimes I worry about her so much and would like to check on her in this way, but if it is 'false' and just a dream then what is the point?

Yes, you can travel in your Astral body to see the real her if you are consciously in the Astral and your psyche and therefore your perception is not being altered by your subconscious (the egos). You will see the Astral counterpart of her physical body. She will be unaware of you unless she is traveling too, but she may remember seeing you in her dreams if she is dreaming herself.

Everything that exists in the physical world also exists in the Astral, so if you throw a shoe on the roof of your house in the physical for example, you can go and see where it landed in the Astral. Then you can find it where you saw it if you check later in the physical.

Now another question that kind of follows from this one. Say I go visit my sister and she wakes up while I'm there, will she see me? Is the Astral body visible to those not in the Astral plane? Or will she maybe 'feel' my presence on some other, non-visual, intuitive level? If I speak to her, will she hear me, or will my voice enter her mind as thoughts?

It's unlikely that she will see, hear or feel you. Things are taking place in the Astral all the time and they are normally not perceived.

That's not to say however that it can't happen, because there are many latent psychic faculties that would allow it to happen. These are increased with the correct techniques, but normally she wouldn't perceive anything.

I just wanted to know if there are any rules that we should follow when in the Astral. I don't want to get there and do something that will offend anyone or anything!

Although you can use your commonsense and intuition, you need to know much more about what's happening in general to know what is best to do and what not to do. Other courses in this series will explain more about this.

If you went to the Astral and saw something like a building that only existed on the Astral, and you described it to me and then I went to look at it, would I see the same thing as you or is the building represented to us based on are own individual experiences and thoughts?

Different people can see the same thing in the Astral because things do exist in the Astral and you can see what is really there. But things can also be put there just for one time, for a teaching for example, or they could just be projections of the mind. That's one of the reasons why it is so important to learn about the psyche and to be free of the subjective projections of the subconscious, of the egos, if you want to have clear and objective Astral experiences.

Week One Exercises

Relaxation and Remembering Dreams

The Weekly Exercises

The exercises on the course are given at the end of each weekly topic. They follow an order, which is designed to be effective for getting results; so to get the Astral techniques to work most effectively, you should do each one of them in the order that they are given.

We begin with two simple ones. The first is a technique to relax the body. The second is one to remember your dreams when you wake up in the morning.

Exercise 1 - Relaxation

It is very important to learn to relax the body for projection to take place. The whole body needs to be relaxed. If you are tense it will be more difficult to focus upon the exercise you are doing and it will be more difficult for the Astral and physical bodies to separate and to fall asleep, as sleep is needed for Astral projection. So this exercise of relaxation prepares you for the exercises that will follow in this course.

This is a very simple technique and can be done easily; it's a matter of relaxing all the muscles in the body.

You need to lie down on your back with your legs straight and your arms by your side.

Go through each muscle, relaxing them all one by one. You can start anywhere as long as you go through each muscle methodically, making each one completely relaxed.

Pay particular attention to the face once you get to it. There can be little areas of tension that are easily overlooked - relax them all.

Once you have checked everywhere, repeat the procedure, just to make sure that there are no areas of tension that you have missed or that have been reintroduced and aim to be totally relaxed.

In this state you are now ready to begin your exercise of Astral projection.

Practice this every night before you go to sleep. When you go to do your exercise of projection you need to relax like this first, so for now do this exercise to get yourself ready for the techniques that will soon follow.

Spend whatever time it takes to relax your muscles, which is normally about five minutes once you learn to do it properly.

Here is a variation on the relaxation technique that you can try:

Relax each muscle of the body by tensing each muscle slightly and then immediately letting it go loose. Go through the whole body this way, paying attention to parts of the body that could be tense.

Exercise 2 - Remembering Dreams

Whenever you wake up from sleeping, try to remember your dreams. This will give you valuable insights about your inner world, it will give you an opportunity to look into your psychology and will get you used to the Astral realm you are going to explore.

It is easy to miss many dreams that have occurred during sleep, but the techniques explained here can help you to remember them. Try them every morning; the more you do them, the more you will develop your ability to recall them consistently. But bear in mind that the clarity of dreams is due to the esoteric work and states of consciousness and, as you go on in this course, you will learn to increase your level of awareness during daily life and so your dreams will become clearer and clearer.

You should work on these exercises diligently and increase your ability to remember.

When you look back over the nights dreams, try to see as many different inner states such as anger, sadness, depression, worries, fear, etc, as you can and see ways you have acted, with what you could consider to be actions that were compelled by these inner states, such as shouting at someone when angry. Look at these different inner states, as much as you are able to see of them.

You may also find dreams that are teachings, which give spiritual information. Look too at the things that take place in dreams and the events that you are in. There may be something that is not obvious, but which you can learn from, particularly if you use your intuition.

There is much to be learnt from dreams; though much is projected by the mind, they can still occur in real places that you have traveled to in the Astral plane within a dream and you can get much information from their scenes, the symbols in them and teachings that may have been given.

Watch for dreams that take place in an environment that is totally unrelated to your daily life. Take note of small details relating to meetings or conversations that you might have had, or anything unusual when relating to other people. Bear in mind the language of the Astral plane is symbolic and you will need to interpret it.

To do the exercise:

When you wake up don't move.

Don't even move a finger. Simply open your eyes and close them again and begin to remember your dreams from the first one you can remember. Try to see it in as much detail as you can; then you may find that more dreams appear. Carry on remembering the ones before if you can. It may take a bit of training not to move when you wake up, but if you try time and again you begin to train your body. It is important not to move when you wake up because by moving the physical and Astral bodies become merged: you become locked into the physical body. Whereas when you just wake up, they often have a looser connection, which makes remembering dreams easier.

Pronounce the mantra Raom Gaom.

If you still can't remember any dreams, continue to lie still for a little while with your eyes closed, to see if they appear. If they don't, then pronounce this mantra. A mantra is a series of sounds, a word or words that have psychic effects. They have these effects depending upon the words or upon the sounds which are often based upon the vowels A, E, I, O, U. These vowels stimulate the Chakras, which are senses of the Astral body. Stimulating them in this way increases certain psychic faculties. Each vowel corresponds to a certain Chakra and increases a particular faculty.

In this case, the mantra for remembering dreams is called Raom Gaom. When you pronounce it, elongate the sound of each letter like this:

Rrraaaaaoooooommmmm Gaaaaaooooooommmmm.

If you pronounce this mentally (not aloud) repeating it over and over again for a while, you'll notice the dreams beginning to appear. As they do, concentrate upon each one. If you need to, pronounce it again several times and try to remember more and so on.

Pronounce
Raom Gaom
internally to
remember dreams
upon waking

You can listen to the mp3 sound file of this mantra by typing the following address into your Internet browser window:

http://www.gnosticweb.com/astralbook/Raom_Gaom.mp3

It will be worth your while to make a good attempt at these two exercises of relaxation and remembering dreams, because they are the starting point and basic foundation in the preparation and education of your physical body and your mind for Astral traveling. You will need to be doing these every day if you really want to experience and investigate Astral travel.

Go Back Into Dreams That Recur

If you see a dream that repeats itself, or see something, be it a symbol, an event, an animal, etc, when you wake up, close your eyes and visualise it. By going back into sleep you can go back into the same dream, but knowing that you are in that dream. In this way, you are consciously self-aware in the dream, in the Astral plane. Then you can explore and learn in that plane consciously.

Imagination is important in this; you need to re-live the dream, feeling that you are actually there in it, not simply thinking about it as though it is something distant.

It is possible to also do this exercise at night as you are going to sleep, praying for help and placing yourself with imagination in a previous dream.

A Dream Diary

You may find it useful to keep a diary where you record your dreams, so that when you wake up and have looked back over the night's dreams, you record them in your diary. It is so easy to forget a dream and you may find that things you don't understand now and would have soon forgotten, may have significance for you later. You can also build an overall picture of your dream life, finding things that are repetitive, prominent or important as patterns emerge over time, but make sure that no one else can see it or find it. This is because someone may find out things that are personal to you.

To begin studying your dreams, try to see what sort of dreams you have - whether you can see any meaning or message in them. It is useful when trying to understand how you function as a person to look for any different psychological elements such as anger or fear you can find and recognize. It is also worthwhile looking to see whether you have been to any places; whether you have been flying (because we can fly in that plane); whether there are any symbols (symbols are a form of communication in the Astral plane) that you can recognize and intuitively capture the meaning of; whether you had any teachings, or even had mystical experiences; or whether the same dream recurs.

If you are in doubt about what you see and don't understand it, try using your intuition to work it out. More information will follow on the courses that will help you to understand them better.

Review how this diary progresses every month, to see how your dream memory has progressed.

Study and analyse these recorded dreams. By using the diary it may help you to spot when dreams recur.

Questions & Answers

Below are some questions that I have answered on remembering dreams:

Q. I find if I come out of a dream that I don't want to leave I just remain still. If I just had a nightmare and don't want to fall asleep into it again I change body positions.

A. That can happen because by remaining still the Astral body has not yet locked into the physical body, therefore you can more easily go back into the dream you just had before you woke up. But as you have experienced, by moving you wake up properly; then you are much less likely to go back into the dream you had before you woke. This applies whether it is a normal dream or a nightmare.

In any case, you are likely to move as soon as you wake up from a nightmare because of the fright. Nightmares are different from normal dreams; they occur in a different place to them.

It is possible to avoid recurring nightmares and also to avoid nightmares altogether. I used to have them, but I don't any more thanks to this work. As you progress in these studies, you will learn more about the Astral and about psychology and you'll eventually be able to prevent them altogether.

Just a little tip for now to avoid the likelihood of having nightmares, to reduce at least one factor that can provoke nightmares: avoid having a large meal before you go to sleep.

Also, taking drugs that alter consciousness increases the chance of nightmares, so for this and many other reasons it's better to avoid them.

Usually when I wake up I can't remember my dreams at all. Is there anything else I could try other than the mantra?

Bear in mind that the technique for remembering dreams needs to be practiced. The memory is trained with it and so it improves with practice. Having just received the exercise of the mantra, you need to give it sufficient time to allow it to work.

Whenever I have a nightmare I always prove to myself in the dream that, "It's only a dream - nothing to worry about."At that point the dream either ends or I gain control of it for a while and it ends soon. What does this mean?

Whenever you have a true nightmare, it's unlikely that you will remember that it's a dream while you're having one. Nightmares are different kinds of dreams with negative creatures or entities or things in them; they have quite a different flavor. In the dreams where you had control, even bad dreams with negative characters in them etc, you were partially awake psychically there. So if you are in a dream and you know that it's a dream, say to yourself that you are in the Astral and jump with the intention of flying. You will see that you can fly and can then travel to different places. If it has unpleasant things in it, you need to use some techniques called conjurations that I will explain soon on the course.

The reason why I can't remember some of my dreams is because they're always so abstract and unstable. The scenery is always warped and constantly changing and so are all the people as well as my emotions. Nothing ever stays

the same for more than a couple of seconds and nothing seems logical or orderly. Please, I hope you can explain this.

You have to take what happens in dreams and the ability to remember them as part of an overall psychological study. The reason why they are so abstract and unstable is because of the state of the psyche itself, as they reflect it.

With the psychological and Alchemical work you will be able to create more order within and have more coherent dreams. They are also related to the level of awareness we have in daily life: the more aware, the clearer the dreams.

I tend to remember my dreams and have been trying to write them down, which I am bad about not doing, but there was one I remember in particular in which I was flying around a very high mountain. I feel pretty sure it was in Tibet or that area. I remember becoming lucid and trying to change direction of my flight. I could not control it and then I lost the dream. Is this common? Is there something I could have done that might have helped me control this experience better or was I just not ready?

Yes, it's very common to lose the Astral like that, particularly if you are not experienced at it. The more you do it the more you learn how to stay there and to go where you want to. Treat it as a learning experience and try to see what happened at the point that you lost it.

Having more awareness while you are there and learning to concentrate when you want to go somewhere will also help, as will the work on transmutation (this is in a later course).

I'm aware that dreams of flying usually are Astral travel, but my most recent one was of flying throughout a gigantic antique store, plus most of my dreams that really have left an impression on me have been dreams that deal with

antiques. Do the antiques have any real significance?

Very much depends on the context of the dream; intuition can usually give you the right direction. That's catching the first feeling you had about the dream when you woke up.

Antiques can be projections of your subconscious, or they can be more symbolic. For example, they could symbolize something ancient that you have to uncover with the spiritual work, or could relate to the state of your spiritual work at the moment.

I was aware that I was in bed, but I was also sitting at the foot of the bed and a being swathed in black (very deep black) came in the room. At first I was rather interested, then fear took over and as it approached me I started to fight it. I remember while doing this, I could not move my real body. I continued to fight and try to speak, but was paralyzed. I finally woke up. This scared me quite a bit. Has anyone else had an experience like this?

Experiences like this are quite common and are well recorded in history. You were paralyzed because you were in the transition period between being awake and asleep, and so did not have movement of the physical body.

What you perceived coming towards you was a sinister entity, taking advantage of your lack of movement. There is nothing to be frightened about though. They can be there at any time; it's just that you were aware of its presence then. Later in the course you will have a technique that you can use to get rid of anything like that.

After reading the exercise, I am not sure how I will be able to do this. I usually wake up with an alarm clock. When it goes off, my first reaction is to slap the snooze button, so once I am awake, I have already moved. In between snooze

button slaps I can usually fall back asleep. What would you recommend I do? I am not sure if I can give up the alarm clock - I would never get to work on time!

It's possible to train yourself to wake up before the alarm goes off, but you may still need to have the alarm anyway.

If you can wake up before the alarm goes off, it's much better and you don't need the snooze button, just the first alarm.

But if the alarm wakes you up, you just have to try the mantra or concentrate so that the dreams can be remembered before the snooze button goes off. The concentration and dream recall can improve the more you practice it.

I awoke one morning early enough to practice the mantra. It seemed to work and I was remembering dreams - that is until I heard a voice so crystal clear that it seemed to be right beside my head in bed. It startled me so much that I jumped away from it almost in a fighting stance to protect myself. My question is, are voices such as this evidence of the Astral?

Yes, they can be from the Astral plane. Because you have been practicing you are more receptive to the Astral and also because you still had a slight connection there, as the Astral body had not quite merged with the physical one. Sometimes higher beings can speak and you can hear them like that. This is different to the voices of the egos, which sound like yells, screams, etc, which are heard as they split from the physical body and go into the molecular world - the fifth dimension.

I just started this course and dreaming is not a problem here. I dream every night and most of the time I remember them. My dreams are crazy ones though. I dream of seeing new homes for my family members, seeing unknown

objects in the night sky and more than once seeing different shapes of stars that move, like foreign objects up there just moving across the dark night sky. I've had that one more than I care to mention. I mostly dream of family and material things we get here on earth. Have you got an answer for these?

At this early stage of the courses, there is still much to learn, particularly about the subconscious and esoteric symbolism. Although it's best for you to find the answers to your own dreams, because they relate to you, you need to learn how to.

It will also help if you now can learn to develop and use your intuition. This can help you to capture the meaning of a dream or an Astral experience. If you see strange things in your dreams, you can use them to wake up in the Astral. Sometimes they are placed in dreams for that purpose.

Can you advise how we are supposed to use the Raom Gaom mantra? Is it something we should repeat as we fall asleep, or first thing in the morning when we wake?

It's something you should do when you wake up. You lie still and close your eyes repeating the mantra in your mind until the dream images appear.

Maybe it's beginner's luck. Last night, I had two lucid dreams, including a flying dream. In the first, I was aware I was dreaming and able to direct it. I was able to focus sharply on things and even read small text, which didn't make much sense. In the second, I was able to fly where I wanted, for a while at least.

My question is - what does this mean? It was a nice experience, and I will try to duplicate it, but what context is there for this and what is the next step? Also, doing the first exercise of remembering the dream before completely

waking up has helped me to retain a good bit of it, though a lot has faded.

You are being helped to learn about the Astral by spiritual beings or by your own Being. If you or anyone makes real efforts to try these exercises you can get a good deal of help.

The next step is to continue with what you are doing and to try the exercises that are going to be given with a lot of patience.

I've been practicing the Raom Gaom mantra for four days, and always yield the same result - I fall asleep again and have another dream.

The interesting part is that I can recall these subsequent dreams easily, as if it was a real life memory from the previous day, and the dreams were mostly a lecture-like session about dreams, fear and feelings. In one of the dreams someone gave me a book on interpreting dreams and he taught me how to read the index and find threads.

From this book I re-discovered a description of my inner fear that has been forgotten for a long time. Is this normal or should I remain awake? I am afraid that these subsequent dreams were only dreams and I haven't actually learned anything.

Even though you are falling asleep you are being taught and are benefiting from it. Keep going with what you are doing and with these courses and you will find that you will learn more and more.

Can you tell me if it is possible to control our dreams? I once had an experience about it. Sometimes I'm aware of my dreams, so when I know that I'm dreaming, I do almost anything in my dream, like by thinking of objects to appear in my hands - there it is - just what I had in my mind. So

can you tell me if it is possible, because I doubted it?

Yes you can do that: what you think of can materialize, but it's not a good idea because then you won't see what is actually there. It's best to be aware, because then you can get real information and teachings, rather than seeing what is in your mind.

Week 2

PREPARING FOR ASTRAL PROJECTION: CONCENTRATION AND VISUALIZATION

*B*efore we look into an actual technique for Astral projection, it is important to prepare the grounds for it, because if you can get the preparation right it will be easier to get into the Astral, and you will be able to go there much more often. Without adequate preparation the techniques given to project are less likely to work.

The determining factors in a person's Astral and dream life are really down to a person's own psychological, inner states. Affecting real change in this, is a whole psychological and alchemical inner work, which is covered in other courses. But both beginners and advanced students can do exercises of concentration and visualization that will greatly assist the ability to Astral project.

43

Concentration

To successfully project it is very important to be able to concentrate on the particular exercise of Astral projection you are doing at the time, without being distracted from it by other thoughts or by anything else.

Willed Astral projection usually occurs when the mind is concentrated at the exact moment that sleep occurs.

Most techniques for Astral projection are variations of concentrating the mind and/or visualizing.

Being concentrated is having the mind and the whole of ones attention on one thing alone.

It is possible to concentrate upon whatever activity we do at one time. That ability is developed by learning to do one thing at a time in daily life. It is also a natural outcome of the psychological work, which I describe in my Searching Within and Journey to Enlightenment courses.

Sitting exercises of concentration train and develop the ability to concentrate upon any Astral or esoteric exercise we do.

Being concentrated upon one thing is different from having the mind completely silenced. There are techniques for silencing the mind; they are not dealt with here because they allow for travel to dimensions above the fifth and are not specific to the subject of this course, which is Astral travel only.

Visualization

Visualization is using the concentrated mind to consciously imagine or remember something.

Visualization has order and structure.

It is possible to actually visualize something that is real, that you know nothing about, if the mind is focused enough. Those who are free enough from the subjective elements of the psyche can use this to look through space, time and dimensions.

The Difference Between Visualization and Fantasy

There is a difference between this kind of visualization and fantasy, although they are similar. With fantasy the mind goes where it wants to without any continuous direction or sustained concentrated thought. What is seen in fantasy is a product of the subconscious and is less effective for projection. Moreover, it feeds the subconscious elements of the psyche adding to the general haphazard scattered mind during the day and adds to the likelihood of having vague and weird types of dreams without meaningfulness in them.

Practicing Sitting Concentration and Visualization

The more the mind is trained to concentrate and visualize the better it becomes at it. It's a matter of practice.

That's why it helps to carry out exercises of concentration and visualization and why they are given so early on in this course.

As you go through the course, you will benefit a great deal in your ability to project if you train yourself daily in concentration and visualization.

Train daily and your chances of projecting will be dramatically increased.

It's like an athlete who prepares for a race by training.

To train the mind to concentrate and visualize you carry out exercises where you sit down or lie down simply to concentrate and/or visualize.

It's very important however not to force the mind. Start with small amounts and gradually build up to a level that you are comfortable with.

When you go to do your exercise to actually project then the mind is already trained to concentrate and visualize and the projection is more likely to succeed.

When trying to practice concentration and visualization or when trying to Astral project, one of the main obstacles is the continuously chattering, daydreaming mind.

The Problem of the Chattering Mind

Many of the failed Astral projection attempts are due to the mind not being trained to be on one thing. It is used to chattering away all day, or it is fascinated in whatever activity is taking place, so that one is not self-aware, which contributes to the chattering. Then when you try to do an exercise to project, the mind carries on chattering. The thoughts that were so active during the day continue to be active and they interrupt the technique that you are doing causing the attempt at Astral projection to fail.

However, when you are aware and concentrated upon whatever activity you are doing in a given moment in daily life, you train and educate the mind to be focused upon one thing and cut down the chatter and interfering inner states (egos), so that when you do your exercise of projection you have a more focused mind and are more able to concentrate upon the exercise, making it more likely to succeed. Working out your framework for your daily exercises, as I will describe later in this course, will help you to carry out one activity at a time and therefore to focus more upon whatever it is you are doing, without thinking about lots of other things at the same time.

It is of course necessary to use the mind - to be able to think and plan, remember things, solve problems, create/invent things, carry out tasks etc, but the problem is that its activity is so compulsive. It just runs of its own accord and it is difficult for it to be on one thing and to be profoundly concentrated for any period of time. It is scattered and the thoughts go on and on, like a wheel turning around and around. It should be a tool that is used; indeed it becomes one if we progress enough on the spiritual path. Ultimately, if you can learn to be in consciousness and to use the mind as a tool, it is possible to direct the mind at will to any task such as projection and to be successful in it. As I mentioned before, there is more information on this psychological work in the Searching Within and Journey to Enlightenment courses.

47

The ability to focus the mind is not something that happens overnight, although it is possible to get it right occasionally in the beginning. It needs to be gradually educated to be on one thing, since it is not used to operating like that. It requires a great deal of practice to train the mind to focus, but it is something that we can start with right away at this stage of the course and which will benefit everything that follows.

If you are not concentrated when trying to project then you will either get taken into sleep by a thought, or will become restless and unable to sleep. Either way, being able to concentrate fixes the problem.

Being able to properly concentrate and visualize is the way to be able to project at will, whenever you want to, as long as there are no other factors such as illness that can stop you. In one night it is possible to project many times, going out into the Astral, coming back, going back out again and so on.

Although it is rare, it is actually possible to Astral project with the eyes open. For example while concentrating upon a candle and looking at it, the concentration can be so intense that with the eyes open you can go out of the body and into the candle.

It could be said that in this case the projection took place while the person was awake, but in fact, even though the physical body has all the signs of being awake, the person did actually sleep - to be awake is to be conscious in that particular body. If we are conscious in the physical body we are awake (although not in a profound esoteric sense) in the physical world. If our consciousness is elsewhere, in another body such as the Astral body, then in reality the physical body is asleep; the consciousness is out of it, even though it may not be normal sleep. Concentration can bring about the processes that take place within sleep that effect projection, even though other, what we would call normal signs of sleep, such as closed eyes, snoring etc, may not be present.

The concentration and visualization exercises given on this course are not the only ones that work. The essential element in them is the concentration. There are many, many variations of concentration and visualization. I have included some on the course that work very effectively, but most variations of visualization or concentration will work as techniques for projection, which is why it is so important to develop these skills at an early stage of this course.

With the ability to concentrate, all the techniques of Astral projection work. Even the mantras which are given later in this course require a degree of concentration to be successful.

Week Two Exercises

Introduction to Concentration/Visualization

There are two types of concentration/visualization exercises we are going to deal with. Each of the exercises has a particular purpose. Both should only be tried for a very short period of time initially, and from then on you increase them gradually in order to train the mind gradually to get used to them.

The two types of concentration/visualization exercises used in this topic are surface and imaginative.

This Week's Exercises

Exercise 1: Surface Concentration/Visualization

This is a technique that enables you to learn to visualize the details of an object and to train yourself to memorize it. This exercise is very useful for the visualization exercises given in later techniques for Astral projection and for your concentration upon the Astral techniques.

Take an object; it can be any object (one popular object for this exercise is a lit candle, but make sure that you only use a candle if it is safe to do so and there is no risk of starting a fire). Sit down and place it where you can see it clearly. Then concentrate upon it in great detail, observing how it looks, the textures, shapes, colors, the material it is made of, the way that light reflects on it, etc, discovering everything you can about it. When you have clearly seen it, then close your eyes and recreate/ visualize the object exactly as it is in your mind. If there are things that you cannot recreate because you didn't look at them properly, or if the image is fading away, open your eyes and

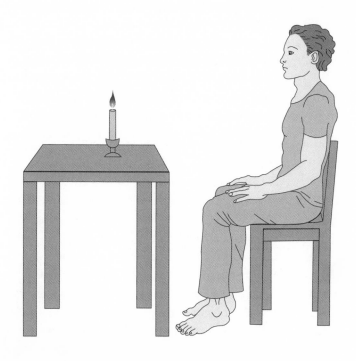

look at it again. Study it, then close your eyes and recreate the image again in your mind. Keep doing this process so that you visualize it as clearly as you can.

This type of exercise gently trains the mind in concentration and visualization, both of which are vital for Astral projection. Try to do it regularly (at least once a day for ten minutes), at a different time from your Astral projection exercise and whenever is convenient for you, but don't do more than 10 minutes. If you want to do this for more times each day then do it, but increase it very gradually, because the mind needs to be educated and trained and you shouldn't force it.

Vary the objects - for example, a glass of water, a plant, flowers, etc, and continue with at least ten minutes each day. Remember to close your eyes when you are recreating the object in your mind and to recreate it often. Don't try to stay there with your eyes open or force yourself to keep staring at the object for a long period of time. Gradually increase the time you spend on this exercise, beginning with just a little.

Exercise 2: Imaginative Concentration/Visualization

This second technique enables you to visualize something you can't physically see.

For this technique, take an object; it can be any object, but for this example we will use a lit candle again. Sit down in a place where you can see it clearly. Then concentrate upon it in great detail using the first technique, observing how it looks, the textures, shapes, colors, the material it is made of, the way that light reflects on it, etc, discovering everything you can about it. When you have clearly seen it, then close your eyes and recreate/visualize the object exactly as it is in your mind. If there are things that you cannot visualize because you didn't look at them properly, or if the image is fading away, open your eyes and look at it again. Study it, then close your eyes and visualize the image again in your mind. Keep doing this process so that you visualize it as clearly as you can.

When you have clearly visualized the object (while having your eyes still closed), imagine, perceive and visualize the inside of the object. In this case go inside the flame and visualize the inside of the flame. Go further exploring anything else you would like to explore about the object. As you are visualizing/concentrating on it, feel yourself being the object - what it feels like being a flame burning on the tip of a wick. At that point you could ask questions to explore the object, such as: What is fire made of? How does it work? What is it for? What is it to be the object? If you pursue the answers far enough you may go beyond what the logical mind can find the answers to.

These answers may not come in the way you expect. It is also worth mentioning that it may not be in your first attempt that you will get the answers to your questions. It may take a lot of work, persistence and patience to really get there, but if you do not dismay and keep going, you will see that you will learn to explore much about things through this very simple, but very powerful technique. On the surface it looks very mundane, but deep down it is spiritual.

You can carry out this imaginative concentration/visualization like this on any object. You could do it with the pen you are holding in your hand at work. You can do it with a flower you have in a vase on your coffee table in your living room, and so on.

Vary the objects - for example, a glass of water, a plant, flowers, etc, and continue with at least 10 minutes each day. You can also try this exercise in a quiet and safe spot in nature and try this imaginative visualization/concentration on a tree, on a rock, the water of an ocean, a lake or a river to mention a few. Remember to close your eyes when you are visualizing it. Don't try to stay there with your eyes open or force yourself to keep staring at the object for a long period of time while observing it. Gradually increase the time you spend on this exercise, beginning with just a little.

Summary of This Week's Exercises

1. Concentration/Visualization
For this week use a lit candle to carry out the surface visualization/concentration for 10 minutes once a day for the first three days of the week.

2. Concentration/Visualization
For your second exercise for this week, carry out the imaginative visualization/concentration on a lit candle for 10 minutes once a day for the last three days of the week.

Remember that if you want to do these exercises for more times each day, then do it, but increase them very gradually.

3. Relaxation
Carry on with your relaxation before going to bed as a preparation for your Astral projection exercise.

4. Remembering Dreams
Continue with the exercise of remembering dreams as soon as you wake up in the morning.

$\mathcal{W}eek$ 3

THE PROCESS OF ASTRAL PROJECTION

$\mathcal{T}$his week we are going to study how to Astral project and will look into what happens when we leave the body, either with Astral projection or with dreams.

The Process of Astral Projection

Every time that we go to sleep, we (the psyche) are leaving the physical body behind and going into the Astral plane of the fifth dimension. This normally takes place unconsciously, but with Astral projection we are simply aware of that process taking place.

To project we normally need sleep, because it is with sleep that the Astral body separates from the physical one. The two bodies are attached by a silver cord that stretches infinitely. It sends messages between one body and the other, which enables the person in the Astral body to go back to the physical body as soon as they wake up from sleep. It is this connection which allows the person in the Astral to unconsciously influence the physical body while dreaming. For example, a person who dreams they are running can move their physical arms and legs and an onlooker can see they are trying to run in their dreams. Likewise, the physical body can influence dreams while asleep. If you stroke someone's hand while they are asleep, they may dream that someone is stroking their hand, etc.

If you have ever had a sensation of falling just as you are going to sleep, what you have been aware of is the Astral body going back into the physical one. However when this happens you have fallen asleep unconsciously and are not aware of splitting into the Astral plane, just the moment of going back into it. The normal process of projecting and coming back to the body is not as alarming as this because you are not caught by such surprise.

When we carry out an Astral projection technique it causes us to go through the process of sleep consciously. We are then aware of all the processes (sometimes just some of them) that take place within the transition period between wakefulness and sleep, until the two bodies separate.

I'll explain how projection works through the use of the techniques.

Techniques for Astral Projection

There are two main types of techniques used for Astral projection – with concentration/visualization and with mantras. I will explain more about mantras in another topic and there will be an exercise this week using a concentration technique for you to try.

I will explain about the process of projection using, as an

example, a concentration exercise – concentrating on the heart. I have found this to be a very good technique to use. The heart is not only a vital organ of the physical body, but in esotericism it also has a spiritual aspect, as a temple or a luminary firmament. However this technique could be substituted for virtually any concentration/visualization technique since whichever type of technique you use the process of projection is very similar.

The first thing you need to do is to get into a position in which you can sleep, lying down in bed for example. That's because it is with sleep that we detach from the physical body. The most effective position to lie down in for projection is on your back, so I recommend that you do that.

Then you need to be able to relax the body (as explained in the first topic) because tension holds us into it. Then, without moving, go straight from the relaxation to your technique for Astral projection.

If you were concentrating on the heart for example, you would direct all your attention to it, as explained in the exercise accompanying this topic.

As you concentrate and the process of sleep begins by staying focused on the exercise, you will be aware of the different processes of sleep as they are taking place – ones that you normally would have been unaware of.

The Process of Splitting from the Body

There are a number of different things, sensations etc, which happen as sleep appears and we leave the body. As you practice Astral projection you may feel all of them, some of them, or none of them, in which case you may just find yourself there in the Astral plane without being aware of projecting.

After relaxing, you may feel that your body becomes very heavy, yet at the same time, strangely you feel very light. As you concentrate on the heart you may find the beats intensifying, a small very high-pitched noise whirring like a motor inside your head, a feeling of not being able to move and then a kind of electric sensation passing through the body. As this happens you may feel yourself rising up, lifting up out of the body. As you lift, you have projected - you're in the Astral.

The sensations of projecting can sometimes be different to the way that I have just described. For example, when you are concentrating you may feel the beats intensifying and as they get stronger, you feel that you're moving with them. The sensation increases as you go higher and higher with each beat, until you rise up out of the body.

Sometimes during the exercise you may get a feeling of immobilization. This is because the two bodies are separating and your voluntary movement of the physical body is being changed for voluntary movement of the Astral body, as you leave the third dimension and go into the fifth. But don't worry, let the projection happen; continue with the exercise and you can eventually float upwards. Don't be distracted from the exercise by any of the sensations that are taking place or you can lose it. If you are sure that you have projected but feel as though you can't move, as though you are paralyzed, then roll over on your side and get up that way.

Stepping Out into Another Dimension

You are then in a completely different dimension. You may find that you have projected just a little way out, lifting up just slightly into the air for example, in which case you may wonder whether you actually are out of the body. So you can check to verify that you have actually projected. To do this, get up from the bed. Do it really, not mentally, but do it very slowly and deliberately, without sharp, sudden movements. Then you'll see that you are in the Astral. Take a look around at the place that you are in, whether the room is exactly like it is normally, if there is anything strange.

If you're still not sure then jump a little in the air and try to fly. If it's the Astral you can fly and a whole new dimension is open to you to explore. Just don't try jumping out of the window or anywhere that is unsafe.

If you have projected higher out of your body, then you know that you're in the Astral, so there are many possibilities open to you. You may wish to explore by walking outside your house and flying, or by traveling to a place that you want to go to. If you want to travel somewhere specific, you could fly there in the same way that you would fly in an airplane here, or you could visualize where you want to go and then go there rapidly, or you could ask a spiritual Being or your own Being to take you somewhere. Sometimes, what you project straight into is what you need to learn from.

As I explained earlier, I found my first experience a bit frightening, going into the unknown, not knowing if I would ever come back. But experience has taught me not to worry. We dream every night; we are in the Astral but nothing bad ever happens to us. We don't get stuck out there because we have a silver cord that attaches us in the Astral body to the physical body. It stretches infinitely long (although there is a limit to how far we can go in the universe, determined by other factors) and is never broken unless we die, which doesn't happen by projecting - it doesn't just snap, nor can we get out and not be able to find our way back. The silver cord always pulls us back. We only have to move during sleep or wake up and we're back in the body.

The difficulty is staying out there long enough. It is so easy to get pulled back. When that happens you usually begin to fade away, or travel backwards at a rapid pace until you fall back into the body, or you just feel yourself merging back with the physical body and you wake up physically.

It can help to hold onto an object so that you are not pulled back so quickly while you are there. It's also important to watch that there are no large emotions or egos such as fear or elation at being there, because these can be enough to pull us back straightaway. You also need to be as aware as possible and to maintain that awareness for as long as you can, because any daydreams there actually turn into dreams and before you know it you're in a dream and you don't realize that you projected until you wake up from sleep.

There is a lot to explain about what you will find in the Astral besides seeing the things that are also here in the physical world. But I would have to explain a lot, too much for this course, which is really about experiencing the Astral plane, so the Journey to Enlightenment course goes into what you will find in the Astral and how you can use it most effectively. Briefly though, it's best to use that plane for your own personal development and spiritual search. There are other beings in the Astral besides humans. There are spiritual beings who have awakened in light and sometimes negative entities who have awakened in darkness. I will explain how these beings of light and darkness are created, what they do and our relationship with them on the Journey to Enlightenment course. I'll be explaining a little about the negative ones and how you can protect yourself from them in another topic soon.

Ten Tips for Astral Projection

1. Astral projection is best done in a relaxed way. Forcing it can interfere with the exercise, so it's important not to force it. Do it for as long as your body allows it. It's better to gradually train the body. Then you become trained to sleep like this instead of falling to sleep in the usual way. Sometimes you may be trying and not be able to sleep; so when you feel that you have tried for long enough, change to a more comfortable position that is better for sleep.

2. It's important to practice the exercises a lot, because it can be difficult to project. The more you try the more you learn about it. Much persistence, patience and dedication is required. You need to keep going every night, even if you have no success for a while - then all of a sudden you may

find that it works. If you don't keep going every day with the exercises then what you have built up can quickly be lost and you have to build up the daily momentum again.

3. Will power is a key element in achieving it; you need to make the effort to push forward, because if you don't you begin to slide down. You need to be persistent and continuous.

4. Get used to doing any of these techniques gradually, particularly lying down on your back if you are not used to it. Start with 10 minutes and then if you feel tired just go to sleep and try again the next time you wake up in the night or early in the morning. It could work at any time. For example, if you wake up just 30 minutes before getting up from bed, it could be the time that works.

5. Don't be afraid of not being able to go to sleep, because this will only be an obstacle for your exercise. It won't let you try the exercise whole-heartedly and your efforts will be wasted.

6. If you feel that you can carry on with the exercise for more than 10 minutes, do so but do not force yourself. Forcing is counter-productive because then you do not feel like doing it the next day as you have experienced discomfort.

7. If you try to project more often it is much better as the body and the mind get used to it without being forced, you enjoy the exercise and you want to do more of it. This is very important because for Astral projection you need consistency, which means you need to try literally every night because that is how you learn how to do the exercise and you can correct whatever you are doing wrong.

8. There is a need not only to make efforts, but also to make those efforts properly. If you don't do an exercise just because you don't feel like it, you will be giving in to laziness and will be far less successful. If you try it sporadically, then you are just fighting the odds and you never go further into the exercise itself, but only hope for a lucky chance. On the other hand, you shouldn't force your body and mind when doing an exercise to the point of agony just because you want a result quickly. As you can see there is a need for a methodical approach to the exercises.

9. Another very useful approach to improve at Astral projection when using any of the techniques of projection, is to try the technique you are going to use to project with for 10 minutes well before going to sleep and trying your actual exercise. This is because you become more familiar with the exercise, so you have less chances of being taken away with thoughts and you know exactly what you need to do for that particular exercise on that night.

10. Astral projection can be a very sensitive exercise. If you do anything out of place the exercise can be over in a split second. By that I mean that during the exercise feelings of fear or excitement or getting involved with the process that is taking place and wanting to almost make it happen by trying to accelerate its process, can make the exercise come to an immediate end. For this reason the exercises need to be done every day so that you see all these obstacles for yourself and know what to do. In this way, with daily practice you learn more about how to do it. Astral projection demands patience and persistence. You need to be prepared to learn from each attempt you make and explore further into the exercise. Then the results will happen seemingly by themselves, sometimes without you expecting it at all.

Problems With Falling Asleep

Concentration also helps with the problem of falling asleep too quickly, which many people who try to project experience. If you fall asleep too quickly and therefore are unable to project, you may find that it helps to learn to go gradually into sleep so that you are more aware going into it, and it is concentration that allows you to do that.

If you have problems of not being able to sleep when trying to project, it's usually due to an over-active mind and a tense emotion (ego) that sometimes eventually arises: this is a consequence of a lack of concentration. Concentration in this case also helps this opposite problem; it then attracts sleep and stops the mind from being over-active, allowing a more successful projection.

Using Breaks in the Night's Sleep to Increase the Chances of Projection

You have a greater chance of projecting into the Astral if you break your sleep and try to project many times at night. The more times you can try this, the more you increase your chances of projecting. It's not a good idea to do this every night for long periods of time however, as in the long run the disturbed sleep will affect you adversely. So a way to do it with the least strain, is to allow an extra hour of sleep when you go to bed and to set your alarm clock to wake up after your normal sleeping hours minus two or three hours. So for example, if you normally sleep eight hours, set your alarm so that you wake up after five or six hours of sleep, then try the Astral again making sure that you get the remaining two or three hours sleep.

When you wake up in each break during the night, get up out of bed and walk around being aware - look at everything in detail; try to keep this awareness and question whether you are in the physical world or the Astral world. Keep this awareness as you go back to bed and then try your Astral exercise.

In study centers, a practice together as a group at three in the morning has proven popular and has produced some very good results. It is not something to do frequently, but it can be alright occasionally for some people. Some groups try it about once a week. Group exercises are especially good for getting successes, as everyone gets together and it creates a strong and positive atmosphere.

Questions & Answers

Q. Are factors like noise (young kids), position of sleep, sharing a bed and age, linked to your ability to Astral travel?

A. Noise and sharing a bed can distract you, but if there is no alternative you have to get used to it and concentrate so that you don't notice it. The position of sleep is the one that you find works best or is practical, but lying on the back works best for most people. Age makes no real difference; it only exists here, but children are less burdened by their egos than adults. As one becomes more involved and caught up with life, one becomes more psychologically asleep, however, this can be reversed and the ability to travel can be increased beyond what it was in childhood.

Since I've started this course I have tried Astral travel a few times. The closest I got was a sense of a small deep black kind of void in front of my closed eyes. This seemed to get larger/deeper filling the whole room. As this happened I would feel (rather than see) 'flashing lights'. However, I would still be aware of things like the TV on or my kids playing in another room. In fact, if anything, I would be even more aware of these distractions. Then

everything would go back to normal. Does this sound like I'm on the right track? Also when trying this I was very aware of my breathing, which sort of distracted me. Should you breathe deep or shallow?

You are getting distracted by things. By learning to concentrate on the exercise, you will forget about the distractions. You should also forget about the breathing if you are not using it to project with.

When you Astral project, how conscious are you of the experience? Would Astral projecting be as conscious as being in the physical body?

Yes, it can be. When you Astral project you are conscious of the experience, just as conscious as being in the physical body. However, there can be times when it is a bit dreamlike, but these are the exception.

Could I have projected and taken off in flight even though trying to move at the time was impossible? I have also flown before, by the way. It is one of the most exhilarating experiences. You come away feeling 10 years younger and so relaxed.

Yes, you could have eventually projected and taken off in flight when you found that you couldn't move. Normally if you can't move, you just wait a little longer and you drift up a bit and can get out, or you could try to see if you could get out by rolling over on your side, then out of bed. But struggling and sharp movements can easily wake you up in the physical.

When do you know it's the right time to try to get up and travel?

If you notice that the Astral body is moving about independently of the physical body; when, for example, parts of the Astral body are moving, the head lifts, a leg rises up, the hands or fingers are moving etc. Then, take a chance and get up gently and naturally. When you get up, jump so that you see if you can fly, to check where you are.

Sometimes you just rise up a little way and you may not feel as though you have projected, but you also need to get up to check. Other times though the projection is obvious, or you already find yourself in the Astral.

When I am trying to Astral travel, I get all these sensations. My mind is fully awake and I feel that my body is dense and unable to move. Am I supposed to fall asleep and then wake up? I have been unable to Astral travel.

You need to continue with your exercise and keep trying patiently every night until you get it, because you are making progress.

You will also do better to pay less attention to the sensations and to concentrate upon the exercise regardless of what sensations are taking place.

You also need to forget that you are falling asleep. Just relax and make sure that there is no anxiety or tension; you can often feel that you are still awake when you have actually projected. So continue with your exercise until there are definite signs of projection itself.

I enjoy the lectures a lot and especially the last one. It led me immediately to an Astral travel again; the best and most convenient one I have had. It was my first but short flight. I have been practicing one year now to consciously project and my efforts were sort of forced, uncomfortable, experiments. I have had many questions, trying to solve all of them by myself, which was not easy. So I consider this course truly precious. The questions that had been

torturing me mostly are:

1. What kept me mostly worried was the lack of control. Why don't I have control of the movement of the Astral body? In the first months it was very difficult to move the Astral body; I was mostly floating above the physical body. Only after one year I started walking a little and flying, and spending more time Astrally.

It's because you need to increase your level of consciousness. This will increase with the exercises on the course and the whole esoteric work. It also improves with experience.

2. Why can't I see clearly?

Again it is due to the level of consciousness/awareness, but it can also be due to the interference from an inner state (ego) or an outside entity. If this happens again use a conjuration (another topic) then you will see more clearly, if this was the problem.

3. What is the reason and the purpose of those loud sounds which resemble the sound of a bird flying? The grosser the sounds the more painful and difficult it was to detach the Astral body. Also, there are strange sensations to be felt on the body, as if streams of something flow, especially on the side of the neck and at the base of the spine (a very uncomfortable push). Sometimes it feels as if the Astral body raises slowly upwards and sometimes it feels as if it withdraws from the lower to the higher parts of the body and then leaves through the head.

You need to be less caught up with the sensations of the body and more detached through concentration. There are symptoms, such as a noise when separation takes place between the bodies, or when the various elements of the subconscious detach and enter the fifth dimension, but worries and thoughts about noises and various sensations can exaggerate them, and it can ruin the exercise. So it's better just to stick to the exercise you are doing (for example, if you are on the heart, concentrate just on that, or a mantra etc) until the moment you are out. Even if you are coming out, don't get caught up with what is happening or the sensations - continue the exercise. And yes, you can go out either way - straight up or through the head.

4. A usual problem was to get stuck in the body and only a few parts detach. It's a real struggle to detach completely.

If a few parts of the body detach, slowly and naturally get up because the split has already taken place.

5. It is very confusing that when I walk Astrally through the house I open the doors normally. How is it possible for the Astral arms to touch and open the material doors? Doors which are closed physically seem to be open and vice versa.

You can open the doors because they are in the Astral and are made of Astral matter, just as we can move things in the physical world with the physical body.

6. When is the best time to Astral project? Usually, I am a little scared to project in the night (perhaps a childhood fear of darkness) so I project during the day, which can be done only during holidays though.

You can project at any time - you just need to sleep. Many people have a great success with an afternoon nap, particularly when they are not too tired when they try. The night has its own advantages though; the atmosphere is quieter and more conducive to mystical things. You do need to overcome that fear though because it's a waste not to be able to project fully at night.

7. In the night I see very poorly, which is a problem. On the other hand, I wonder how I see and perceive the light since the Astral eyes don't function with the light as the physical ones. Is there any way to perceive the places

and objects more clearly, with more light?

The Astral eyes see Astral things just as the physical ones see physical things, so you can see things just as clearly there as here. Clarity in the Astral is due to the level of consciousness/awareness, the interference of entities, psychological states and what is being shown. Also the consciousness can be woken up by spiritual beings when they need to teach or show something.

I'm currently doing the course and had an interesting experience last week that has given me quite a lot to think about. I would appreciate your thoughts and any advice you may have regarding this matter.

Firstly, and quite fortunately, simple self-observation is something I have been practicing for over a year now and can appreciate how self-awareness here would translate to the Astral.

About six months ago, I recognized I was having recurring dreams. One night I was even able to redirect a dream by thinking, "No I'm not going there tonight," and I didn't. These are not bad dreams or nightmares by the way.

After last week's lecture, when I went to bed I was beautifully relaxed, concentrating on my heartbeat, when suddenly I thought "(main content of dream)" and that instant the buzzing symptom began with great intensity. It was quite remarkable. (Although I am quite familiar with the buzzing sensation, I find it really uncomfortable and I am trying to work through what I believe is fear, which prevents me from completely separating.)

I dislike the buzzing sensation so much that, in this instance I put my fingers in my ears in an attempt to dull it. After a short period of this I gently returned to my heartbeat, and with great hilarity realized that it was my

Astral body with which I had tried to block my ears, etc!

To me, there are two issues that stand out; one - the thought connection to a previous dream event that clearly became a trigger to commence separation, which has never occurred with me before, and two - (although I haven't got to your lecture on intuition) the feeling I get is that there is something I need to learn further by dealing with this dream/issue in the Astral, even if it is to simply determine whether it is additional egos making mischief.

Fear, avoidance and denial seem to be the obvious egos in this experience. So, if for the time being I set these aside, my curiosity and enthusiasm is fired, fear allayed, and I have room to develop more courage needed to actually separate, hopefully with the potential to learn something, which I feel may just hold something of deep significant importance to me.

Thank you for you for providing simple access, and presenting this and other Gnostic matters with a responsible approach.

The decisions you make in the physical regarding what you are going to do in the Astral translate into the Astral that very night, so you may find yourself doing or not doing them, depending on what you decided.

Concentration on the heart is a very powerful exercise. If you have been very relaxed and concentrating on your heartbeats, it is very likely that your concentration on the heart triggered off the steps for real Astral projection, to the point you were out of your body and closed your Astral ears. You simply missed the separation as you may have drifted in and out of sleep.

There is certainly a lot to learn from dreams; it is very good that you are using your intuition for your dreams. It could be the case that in that dream you are being shown aspects of yourself, or something that you need to be aware of. That is something for you to decipher with the help of your intuition and looking into your life as you live it.

Fear of the unknown is very common in life. There were a lot of things in life that were the subjects of our fear, but we got on with them and now we do not even remember to be afraid of them. Think of a piece of fruit that you do not know of, would you eat it? Your answer would be "no", but a person who knows the fruit will eat it and even enjoy it with no thought of fear. Experience and knowledge help a great deal with that type of fear. Having some initial courage you can begin to open many doors.

Every time I try to Astral project I lie there for a long time and I feel things, but I never seem to make it.

You need primarily to develop concentration. If you are feeling all sorts of Astral sensations, try to get up out of bed like you would in the morning. It's not always true that we project into the air when we split. We sometimes split but remain on our bed, feeling like we are still not split. So then, you need to carefully get out of bed and take a little jump to float - you may get a pleasant surprise.

I get to the point which I believe is right before separation, but I still see only blackness. Then I start worrying about my eyelids and wonder if I am supposed to somehow see through them upon projection.

This is a common problem. You won't normally see through your physical eyelids. If you are in the Astral you need to open them. Very occasionally when trying to project we can suddenly seem to 'see through our eyelids', but then we are in the transition period between the two dimensions - the physical body has its eyes shut and the Astral body is seeing. This passes when the full split has taken place.

Try not to confuse the functions of the two bodies: the physical body and the Astral body. Once you feel you have separated, I would suggest firstly getting up out of bed carefully as you would in the morning, perhaps just sitting on the bed and then open your eyes just as naturally.

When I try to relax in bed and concentrate, I almost always fall asleep. Am I doing something wrong or do I just need more practice? One more thing, my episodes of Astral travel that just happen often happen if I have stayed up much later than normal and am very tired.

It is very common to fall asleep as the exercise begins. This is because your mind needs to be trained to be on one thing. Otherwise, you fall asleep with the initial thoughts, which then become dreams immediately. You just need more practice, and as you practice the exercises more, you will learn to go further into the transition period between wakefulness and sleep. It is in that transition period that conscious Astral projection takes place. Sometimes, if you are in that transition period you may think you are awake, but in fact you could even be snoring with a very light sleep, so that you cannot even hear yourself snoring.

Sporadic Astral experiences can be the result of being helped spiritually, so that you learn to do it by yourself and in this way, you are taught and encouraged.

Whenever I practice the exercises I never seem to fall asleep; when it doesn't work I just get up. Does this mean I'm not relaxed enough or am I too aware of what's happening?

In Astral projection it usually means that you need to develop the ability to focus the mind on one thing. If you do, you will find that you are able to actually attract sleep.

I think I had my first Astral experience. But I cannot be sure it was Astral travel. Is there a possibility of dreaming of Astral travel? The reason I ask is because in the middle of the night I sort of 'woke up' and began to feel the vibrations. I thought, "OK - this time I'm going to concentrate on my heart beat." Sure enough, the vibes got deeper and more powerful and I felt I had projected (I had cast a circle before also).

After flailing around in my Astral body unsure of how to use it for a few moments, I was able to get up and walk around the house. I did the conjuration of Jupiter everywhere just in case. Then I tried to go outside my window and I was unable. I thought, "Enough of this - I'm doing it" and took a run and jumped through the wall in my living room, and ended up sort of flying outside. I tried to fly to my girlfriends' house, tried to fly a little way down the road. This is where my memories stop.

My question is that it wasn't nearly as vivid as I'd been led to believe or expected it to be. Also, it happened in the middle of the night, some time after I'd fallen asleep from trying the exercise. I can't be sure I was fully conscious, and even during the experience it felt like I was a little out of it. Do you have tips or explanations? Also - how do I make the experience more vivid, like daily consciousness or even more so?

It is good to see that your efforts are paying off. It was an Astral travel experience and you did very well in your first go.

The technique of the concentration on the heart helps with Astral experiences generally because it is the Chakra (a sense of the Astral body) that helps Astral travel and is an important spiritual center. You can get benefits from it not just of projection but also by being woken up in your dreams, or having a very vivid dream with very useful information for you own work, or you can be woken up in the middle of the night to try again and you took advantage of the latter.

There could be many reasons why your experience was foggy; one is that you need more experience. As you try more and more, you will get better at it. However, you need to get more experience in daily awareness of the moment and your level of consciousness needs to increase in the physical world for your experiences in the Astral to be more vivid and clearer. Some people experience a vivid Astral projection as a help, so that they know what it is like, but in your case you have been given information in the experience itself to do more than just try the technique for Astral projection. That is, you need to make efforts to do the exercises like the jump for waking up in dreams, which will help you make the experiences more vivid and more conscious.

However, ultimately, the information on the Searching Within course and the Journey to Enlightenment course will enable you to have Astral projection experiences far beyond what you can imagine. And more importantly, you will be able to acquire esoteric knowledge that will be given to you because you got there consciously and by your own efforts.

How do I get my eyes open when I'm in the Astral?

It is quite common to be unable to open your eyes at the beginning, as you are not used to the Astral plane or your Astral body. This, as when the Astral is dark even if your eyes are open, can also be due to the state of the consciousness (which is not clear or lucid enough at the time), or due to the influences of negative entities or negative inner states. There are techniques called conjurations that are given on this course, which you can use which help to get rid of those negative influences.

This question might sound a little bit weird. I don't know if it's got anything to do with Astral projection or not, but before I Astral projected for the first time a few months ago, I heard singing. It was a woman singing, although I couldn't make out what she was singing. It was as if it was far away in the distance, and it was definitely not outside my head (this sounds weird), but I had to listen inwards to hear it. Do you know what this means?

You can hear sounds from the other dimensions; this is called clairaudience. You usually hear them in the transition period between wakefulness and sleep. It indicates that you were probably assisted in your projection.

Voices of a different kind can also be heard in that transition period before going into the Astral or sleep; these come from the various parts of the subconscious (egos) when they are leaving the physical body to go into the fifth dimension. They sound like shouts, moans and babble. These were not the ones you heard at that time, but it's worth knowing about if it happens to you in the future.

Week Three Exercises

Concentration/Visualization on the Heart

This Week's Exercise

A Technique for Astral Projection: Concentration/Visualization on the Heart

This week we are going to look at concentrating on the heart. I have found this to be a very good technique to use. It is one of the main techniques for Astral projection.

The heart is not only a vital organ of the physical body, but in esotericism it also has a spiritual aspect.

We are going to look in detail at two different techniques - concentration on the heart beats and visualizing the heart. The two techniques when practiced, improve the quality of your dreams and are an efficient way to learn to Astral project. These techniques are not limited to one's bed or practice room alone. They can be practiced almost anywhere you have the opportunity to. What is important is to practice and to learn to do them well so that you succeed with them.

Technique 1:
Concentration on the Heart Beats

After lying on your back and relaxing, begin this exercise by gently perceiving your heart beats. If you cannot perceive them, take three deep breaths and you should feel your heart beats almost straight away. If you can't feel it you can imagine it beating. Once you begin to notice the beats, concentrate on each of them. Keep focusing on your heart beats and try to feel them throughout the body until your whole body is a heart beat. You can also do this by directing the beats of the heart to the various parts of the body. For example, you could direct the beats of your heart to the tip of your nose, the palms of your hands, the soles of your feet and so on, until eventually you feel that your whole body is a heartbeat.

When concentrating on the heart using this week's techniques, remain in the same position until you Astral project. Don't try to get up when you feel the first signs of the Astral split beginning to happen. Continue with your exercise until you actually project, usually by rising up or floating up out of your body - at that stage you get up and move around.

Technique 2:
Visualization/Concentration on the Physical Heart

For this technique you lie down on your back on your bed or on the floor, or sit down comfortably on an armchair. Once you are relaxed, direct your attention to your physical heart with the purpose of visualizing it within your own physical body. Begin by gently concentrating on the heart and visualizing it in detail: its shape, size, color, etc. Next, further explore in detail other areas of the heart like the texture of the heart muscle, surfaces, the chambers, the arteries attached to the heart, etc. As you explore the inner and outer parts of the heart try to find out how it works, what it is made of and what it is for. Carry on exploring the heart until you Astral project.

An Extra Optional Point for Visualizing the Heart in Stages

The concentration/visualization on the heart can bring good results if you learn to visualize the heart in stages. In your first attempt you may wish to explore the outer part of the heart only and try to get that part right. In your second attempt you may still need to do that. Your next exercise could be exploring the chambers of the heart. Later on you may wish to explore the arteries attached to the heart and so on. When using this progressive technique you should always retrace all the stages you have already learned to visualize. In other words, you keep progressing by visualizing more and more areas of the heart, but always retrace what you have learnt to visualize before until you cover the whole heart. It is important to aim to explore your heart in depth.

This technique for Astral projection can work more effectively if you do a 10 minute exercise of visualizing your heart well before your Astral projection exercise. This way you familiarize yourself with the technique and you gain experience of how to do it before you actually try to Astral project with it.

For this particular technique you must remain in the same position until you Astral project.

Below are some tips that may ease your road to the experience and help you to succeed at Astral projecting with the above techniques. Some of the following tips have already been mentioned in the topic for this week.

Useful Tips to Succeed in Astral Projection with Concentration on the Heart

1. A good relaxation will make your attempts at Astral projecting easier. Take time and care in learning how to relax your body and see which areas are most tense in your body so that they are relaxed when you start your Astral projection exercise. Check that tension hasn't crept back into your body when you start your visualization exercise or any other exercise for Astral projection, as this will lock you into your physical body, preventing you from Astral projecting.

2. Learn not to scratch an itch in your body. If you scratch it, it will spoil your exercise. You need to learn to ignore it. It is difficult at first, but if you train yourself not to scratch an itch, you will have far less exercises spoiled by them. Many exercises can come to an end in this way and often it is very hard to get back into the same stage of Astral projecting once you have moved to scratch yourself.

3. Once you begin your relaxation exercise try not to move from that moment on. Remain still during your exercise for Astral projection.

4. When you are using a visualization technique to project with, try not to get distracted by the sensations or noises that occur with the process of the split, as this can also bring your exercise to an end. Ignore those sensations and carry on with your visualization as though nothing is happening. If you get sidetracked with the process that is taking place, that is as far as you are likely to go. You are going to get stuck with whatever you got distracted with.

81

5. When you notice that you have reached the sleep paralysis stage where you feel you have been immobilized, continue with your exercise and try not to move at all because you are very close to Astral projecting.

6. Don't get distracted by background sounds unless there is something urgent to attend to. Concentrate upon your exercise of projection.

7. It is very important that you let the process of Astral projection take place without you trying to speed it up or stop it. Do your exercise concentrated at all times. This is all you need to be concerned about. If you do it this way, the rest will take place as a result of your good concentration and visualization of the exercise.

8. Make sure you do your exercise determined to be successful. Be clear that if you do your exercises methodically there is little reason why you should not be able to Astral project. It will spoil your exercise of Astral projection if you do it just for the sake of doing it, without being determined to be successful. You must be determined to make it. Don't let your laziness get in the way.

9. Be ready to learn from each attempt you make at Astral projection and learn to correct the mistakes you detect you are making, because that will bring you much closer to success.

10. The times you have failed in the attempts you have made to Astral project only add to your experience. You do not only learn from your successful Astral projection attempts but also from the ones in which you have failed, if you are ready to learn that is.

11. Don't give up on your attempts to Astral project. Remember the more you try it the more chances you have to experience Astral projection.

An Alternative Technique: Visualizing the Heart as a Spiritual Place

Finally, there is a variation on visualizing the heart, by visualizing it as a spiritual place. This can bring benefits associated with the heart's spiritual aspects.

Here are two variations of that exercise, which you can try some time in the future:

Visualizing Your Heart as a Temple - Direct your attention to your heart and visualize it being like a temple, a place with light and with the layout of a temple as you imagine or know one to be.

Visualizing a Forest in the Heart Region - Direct your concentration to the heart region and visualize thunder and lightening. Imagine clouds traveling at rapid speed, driven by powerful winds disappearing on the horizon. Imagine gigantic eagles flying throughout the sky, deep forests full of life and sunshine. Imagine the singing of birds and the sweet and gentle chirping of crickets in the forest. Next, imagine and visualize a golden throne in the forest where a female spiritual Being, a very divine lady, is seated. Fall asleep visualizing all of this.

Summary of This Week's Exercises

1. Concentration/Visualization
Carry out a 10-minute visualization of the heart daily, well before your Astral projection exercise. Don't worry if at first you cannot visualize much at all. As you keep going you will learn to visualize the heart more and more.

2. Astral Projection
This week try to Astral project by concentrating on the heart beats. For this exercise you need to carry out your relaxation exercise first and then move on to your exercise for Astral projection.

3. Remembering Dreams
Now that you are doing exercises of Astral projection, it is even more important that you try to remember your dreams first thing in the morning. The mantra for remembering dreams is Raom Gaom.

You pronounce it elongating the sound of each letter like this: Rrraaaaaoooooommmmm Gaaaaaoooooommmmm.

4. Don't forget to increase the length of your exercises gradually.

Concentration/Visualization on the Heart

Q. Every time I try to Astral project it's really easy for me to relax my whole body. Then after I get the vibrations I always seem to make it to the point of the split, but then immediately my heart starts beating really fast and intensely. I always try to ignore it but it's too intense to ignore. It feels like my heart is going to blow up out of my chest! This usually stops me from making the split (although sometimes it's my chattering mind). I know for a fact that my heart doesn't beat like that because of any emotions like fear or nervousness, because I'm always very calm and concentrating hard. It's like a physical thing that comes out of nowhere. So is there any reason why this keeps happening and how do I prevent it?

A. Try sticking to concentrating on the heart - then it doesn't matter how much it beats. Once you get used to doing it then try it with the other exercises. If there is no emotional state involved it will go back to normal.

Should we keep trying to concentrate until we eventually fall asleep? I just started the course and I've

been concentrating for about 15 minutes then giving up and going to sleep on my side. I have the time to do it longer, just never have. Also for some reason, I just cannot visualize the heart for more than five seconds... I can concentrate on my heartbeat but it's a quiet beat unless I take deep breaths. Any advice is welcome thanks.

It is best to increase it gradually. If you are comfortable with 15 minutes then go on to 20 and so on. In this way you are going to train your body and mind at concentration very well, and you are not going to be disrupted by discomfort of any kind.

It is normal to last very little time concentrated on the heart. This is because the mind is not trained to focus on anything for long at all. You will see that as you carry on with your exercises regularly, your span of concentration will increase.

Going into the details of how your heart looks like through visualizing it, naturally increases the heartbeat. Try this; it works very well.

I've been trying to Astral travel several times now and I can feel myself getting close. I've even had some of the experiences mentioned in the lecture, but before I get anywhere I lose concentration on my heart either because my heart rate becomes more shallow and it's really difficult to concentrate on it, or I become distracted by my own breathing. Can you please give me some advice on what to do?

It helps to imagine the heart; then you can keep focused on it better. With practice you don't lose it like this.

Once you feel the heart beating then visualize and concentrate on the heart, forgetting about the breathing, letting it return to normal. If you think about breathing at any time, go straight back to the heart. Eventually with some practice, the distraction from the breathing will subside. It's a small ego that is affecting you.

I've tried to Astral project numerous times and still no success. I can relax my body to the point where my body is tingling, almost as if it has fallen asleep, like what happens when you sit on your foot for a long time, but after that nothing. Sometimes, this feeling gets really severe and my body feels like it's contorted into odd positions even though I'm just lying on my back. This also is hard to explain. One time, while I was trying to project, I was in steady relaxation for about 15 minutes and during the other five minutes my body felt like it was sideways even though I was lying on my back. Is this my Astral body moving, or am I doing something wrong? Are there any dietary precautions I should be taking?

I have the same problem about the heartbeat being too faint and becoming obscure because of the breathing. Should breathing be a conscious effort? I mean like, 1...2...3...4, hold...1...2...3...4.

Once you relax, you need to concentrate on the exercise without paying attention to the sensations that are happening.

When your body felt like it was sideways even though you were lying on your back, your Astral body had already split. This was your Astral body moving, although other parts of the Astral body can also move separately from the physical body. Next time, slowly get up from the bed and you can find yourself in the Astral. You were not doing anything wrong - you were very close.

As far as dietary precautions go, the main thing is not to eat a heavy meal before you sleep.

When the heartbeat becomes too faint and obscure, you should visualize it and you will find it again. Once you do, then return to normal breathing. With practice you don't lose it like this.

Sometimes, when trying the exercise, I start feeling a heaviness, almost a pressure in my head and I start feeling as if I am being tilted in a circular motion and I feel dizzy. I can carry on, but I have never got beyond this and I never feel as if I have fallen asleep. Am I doing the exercise correctly? Also, can you concentrate on breathing? Because sometimes breathing blocks the feeling of the heart beating.

If you feel as though you are being tilted and are moving in a circular motion and this is quite noticeable, you can try slowly getting up from the bed to see if you are in the Astral, because you may just catch the moment after you have split. But if you are not quite there, it's important to concentrate on the exercise you are doing: that focusing of the mind will bring about the split.

If you are concentrating on the heart, forget about the breathing; let it go on normally and stay just with the heart. You can concentrate on the breathing alone as an exercise if you want to experiment with that, but remember to stick just to that. Don't switch between it and the heart or anything else, or you may easily spoil the exercise.

I tried relaxing my body. The heartbeat was there and I could feel my heartbeat even shake the bed in rhythm, but when I tried to project there was nothing. Are you asleep when this happens or are we in that in-between stage of sleep and awake? Maybe I'm trying too hard.

It's not that you are trying too hard, but you are getting too physically involved with the heartbeat. You won't then be able to sleep and sleep is needed for the projection (watch you don't get emotionally involved either, with tension for example).

Make sure you carry out the relaxation exercise first of all. Then concentrate on the heartbeat, but relax into it. Try also to visualize the heart a bit more when you do it. You may find that other exercises like mantras help you to relax more into the projection, until you learn more about how it works.

Don't give up on the heartbeat though, because with a bit more practice you could get somewhere with it. It can take a lot of patience and persistence to get it.

We are in that in-between stage of sleep and wakefulness when the splitting of the Astral and physical bodies takes place, but as soon as you have projected, the physical body is asleep.

I keep practicing the exercise, except I place my hands on my chest to better feel my heartbeat. Should I do this? Also, my heart does beat faster and faster, but then it feels like I have to fight to breathe, which usually breaks my concentration. What should I do?

First of all, you need to get your hands off your chest because it is distracting you and you are becoming too involved with it.

Secondly, as you start the practice relax and go gently into the practice. When you begin to feel your heart beating, carry on as though your heart has always beat that way and keep your concentration on the practice. Then, you will feel the first signs of Astral projection.

However, once the signs appear again you need to be concentrated in the practice and not get involved in what is happening. This is very important, because with your excitement or your fear you either get stuck at one point or the exercise will come to an end.

Keep going - you are not very far from achieving it.

I just tried the heartbeat exercise. I asked for divine

89

help to keep my mind clear and focused, to keep evil away, and to assist me in projection. I laid down and relaxed my body twice. Then I focused on my breathing. First, I felt the beating in my ears. Then my feet up to my calves tingled and the tips of my hands. After that, I was hearing the beating in my chest. Then I felt this circular motion in the center of my chest near my heart, my feet, and my hands. Then I only remember waking up; I didn't get to the jumping part. How am I progressing? What was this? Was it just in my mind or what? Should my eyes be open or closed?

You are getting there; you were splitting into the Astral when you woke up.

Try to keep going with the exercise no matter what is starting to happen to you due to the splitting. Watch out for emotions too because they can easily wake you up.

You should have your eyes closed, as sleep will arrive better and you are less likely to be distracted.

How do you know when to stop concentrating on your heartbeat and know you're out of your body?

When you actually lift up out of your body.

Since I heard in the lesson about concentrating on the heartbeat, I tested it nearly every day. In the evening I always fall asleep, so I tested in the afternoon, which gave me some more results, but I only get some of the first things you describe - beeps in the ear and feeling heavy. Are there any other techniques, which are a little more effective?

It sounds as though if you keep continuing with this one you will get some results. There are exercises that suit some people better than others however, and as you go through the courses you will get different ones. It's a matter of trying them and being very patient.

In general I have always been a light sleeper and maybe that is why I am finding Astral projection difficult. What is the most important feature in reaching the Astral: sleeping on the back, listening to the heartbeat or relaxation? I never sleep on my back, but I am trying to train myself. I am also blocking outside noise, but I haven't made much progress. Is the main point of listening to the heartbeat to block out the subconscious thoughts and day dreaming so that they don't mask the Astral?

You should try to get all three right. You can be in any position that is comfortable, but lying on the back is the most effective one for most people. The thing that helps Astral projection most is concentration, concentrating fully on the exercise that you are doing. That is why it is important to practice it with the exercises on this course and to concentrate upon what you are doing during the day.

I have been doing the concentration on the heartbeat exercise. I have been doing it and all of a sudden, a rushing to the head feeling happens and then I feel like I am floating above my body. It is quite a pleasant, releasing feeling. I can't see anything but black. I still have my eyes closed. Should I try opening them or will that break the exercise?

You should open your eyes when you reach that stage, because you have already gone into the Astral. It will only break the exercise if you do it before you split.

I've tried to concentrate on my heart in both the lying and sitting positions, but I am getting no joy. At moments I can feel it ever so slightly flutter, but mostly I can't feel a

thing. What am I supposed to be sensing? Am I supposed to be sensing anything? If however, I hold my breath, I do feel it pounding in my chest. What should I do?

You need to be visualizing the heart, even if you can't feel it very well. The more you do this, the more you will gradually begin to feel the heart. Later on you will feel your heart as soon as you concentrate on it, but getting visualization right is the key to it. Maintaining the visualization will enable you to project with this technique.

It is important to practice visualization for at least 10 minutes a day; the more you do it, the more you will explore your heart and get interested in what the heart is esoterically. Visualization will also help you in any other Astral exercise that you do, because you learn to focus the mind.

Week 4

THE INFLUENCE OF THE PSYCHE

This topic explains the relationship between the state of the psyche and dreams and Astral travel.

It outlines the structure of the psyche: the mind, consciousness, emotions, feelings and personality, and shows how they affect what is dreamt and what is experienced in the fifth dimension.

Finally, it explains what parts of a person are present in the different dimensions.

This will allow a greater understanding of what to do and what to take into account psychologically when exploring the fifth dimension.

The State of the Psyche

It is the state of the psyche that is the determining factor in what is experienced in Astral travel, dreams and out-of-body experiences.

That is why it is so important to understand the psyche and the different factors that affect Astral and dream experiences.

To have value, these kinds of experiences need to be both objective and meaningful.

By objective I mean that what is experienced is something true, real and not simply a projection of one's own subconscious.

By meaningful I mean that the experience is of value in a spiritual sense. I use the word spiritual here to include the search to discover important information about oneself, life, the way things work, etc.

To look at the different parts of the psyche in order to understand it more, I have included below a summarized version of some information that is taken from the Searching Within course, for those who have not yet done that course. If you have done the Searching Within course, you will know already what I am referring to.

After the information on the psyche I will explain about the different parts of the psyche in the different dimensions. If you take this information and begin to observe inside yourself, you will then begin to explore your psyche and will see how it works and how it relates to the Astral plane and dreams.

To explore inner transformation and spiritual development further, you will benefit from the extra information given on the Journey to Enlightenment course.

The Components of the Psyche

The psyche consists of three main components:

The subconscious or egos - which are the thoughts, emotions, instincts and feelings. They have their roots in, and common parts with the animal kingdom.

The consciousness - the essential part of what we are, what is 'awake' and contains all the spiritual qualities.

The personality - what we acquire within one life, the means of expression for the first two. It contains skills we learn, like driving a car, typing, etc.

I'll outline these main components starting with the subconscious.

The Egos – the Subconscious

The psyche is predominantly composed of a multitude of psychological elements such as desires, drives, impulses, negativity, pleasures and self-centered states that unceasingly come and go. In modern Gnosis they are called 'egos' but they could just as easily be called selves, or I's (as Gurdjeff called them) or psychological adjuncts. I find that 'ego' is the simplest term to use, as there is no definitive term used in everyday terminology.

We sometimes say that a person has a strong ego, but in reality each person contains a multitude of different inner states, which all have the continuity of the feeling of 'I' or 'me' in common. At one time someone may be full of pride, or anger, or jealousy, or fear for example, but soon afterwards that state can be gone only to be replaced with another. One enters, then another, and so on endlessly. An inner state is rarely the same for long, unless they are particularly powerful that is. Then ones such as fear or depression may last for a long time.

There are many inner states (egos) that everyone would feel better off without. There are psychological states that make life miserable, such as worries, stress, depression, fear, etc, and there are states that cause harmful actions such as stealing, violence, fraud, gambling, arguments and so on. The multiple egos constitute the subconscious.

All of them can be observed, understood and eventually removed. You may think that they are permanent parts of you and are necessary for your functioning; however it is not true. Each human being has the capacity to observe and then remove them and to replace them with a different way of being, with the qualities of consciousness such as intelligence, wisdom and love. With the egos there is no peace; they have to be absent for true peace to occur.

The egos are based upon those psychological things needed by animals for their survival. That is why some human behavior often looks animalistic.

They manipulate each person as a robot would be by a program. They are nature's program which keeps the animals locked into a program of behavior, so that they can survive and be part of the whole natural process, without any need or wish for self-conscious activity. That program of nature forms the basis of human behavior.

That's why amongst people there is so much greed, anger, argument and war. Each person is struggling to find their way in life, with no real purpose to it – driven by nature's program.

There is so much within a person that is unknown to them or shut off from them. As you observe inside and eliminate the different egos, you see more and more of what is within, in its various levels of complexity. In this way you gradually begin to be conscious of the parts of the subconscious and, with further techniques, to increase the level of consciousness.

Often these different states that are normally shut off from everyday life are seen in dreams, where the norms of society are taken away and the subconscious roams, living out its fantasies, its pleasures, its fears, etc.

By looking into dreams, the reality of the psyche is laid open.

There is no use in trying to hide from the reality of what is within. The thing is to see what is within and to eliminate whatever egos there are.

In dreams the subconscious elements (egos) are free to roam and project their scenes onto the Astral world, which then form the dreams. Therefore, the more egos that are eliminated the freer the person is from their influence and the dreams and Astral experiences become clearer and more objective. This reduction of the subconscious also affects waking life in the three-dimensional world. The less a person is submerged in the subconscious, in the egos, in daydreams, the more aware they are of the present moment they live in.

The levels of awareness and daydreaming during daily life are directly related to the levels of consciousness and subconsciousness while dreaming when asleep. The more awake, aware, objective and free of the subconscious a person is during the day, the more awake, aware, objective and free of the subconscious a person is during the night in the Astral.

The Personality

Let us go on to the next component, the personality. This constitutes what is acquired in the normal course of development in one life. It is formed by the age of seven and by then we are recognizably the person we are today; even though we may have changed in many ways, we are recognizably the same person as then.

The personality is a vehicle for the egos and consciousness to express themselves; it is formed by the experiences of life and includes all the skills that are acquired, such as walking, reading, talking, etc. Without this, the raw consciousness and egos would not be able to function in the world. These latter two exist from life to life, whereas the personality in formed in one life and is discarded thereafter.

Each personality develops uniquely according to the circumstances of the person's upbringing; the place and era of birth, the parents, family, the egos, etc, affect its development.

Different personalities have different egos that predominate. When it is said that someone has a proud personality for example, it is not the personality that is proud but that the personality is a vehicle or the means through which the ego of pride expresses itself, perhaps through mannerisms or words or gestures.

Each of us has a different personality because it is shaped by our early experiences in life, such as what our parents taught us, the school we went to, the friends we had, the books we read, etc, but it is useful to us only for one lifetime and is acquired only in one lifetime. Once this present life is over, it is discarded at death and that personality gradually disappears as the physical body disintegrates in the grave.

These personalities of the deceased are what people commonly refer to as ghosts. They are personalities left behind by people who passed away. That is why they are normally found in places where the deceased used to live. They exist in the fifth dimension and are formed from mental matter; they gradually dissolve with time after death.

The personality is needed to be able to function in this world and to interact in life, but it is the other two, the consciousness and the egos, that are the most important when considering travel in the Astral plane.

Consciousness

Consciousness is the spiritual part, the immortal essence of a person. All spiritual growth, true wisdom, intelligence, love, peace and mystical experiences take place within the consciousness.

It submerges into the subconscious during sleep, emerging at different times to be in dreams. Consciousness gives the awareness of the present moment.

Awareness of the present moment during the day is related to the level of awareness at night in dreams or in the Astral plane.

Acting and responding to the world with consciousness is the highest way of being. When we respond to a situation with this, its faculties are active and the response is intuitive and intelligent. By seeing you comprehend without the complications of the mind and the egos. This applies to things outside oneself, or to the study of the psychological aspects within oneself.

With consciousness sufficiently developed the mind becomes a tool for it to use. Consciousness contains all the psychic faculties such as intuition, clairvoyance, telepathy, ESP, etc.

Being aware is the right state for any given situation; then we are able to respond to it correctly, without the bias of emotions, or rigid points of view, etc. When we are freed from the subjective viewpoints of the egos, we are free to see reality as it is. The greater the percentage of awakened consciousness, the greater the ability to perceive reality.

Consciousness is manifest with awareness, by being aware of the information from the five senses and/or aware of what is happening within psychologically; then the consciousness is activated. By being aware we live in the present moment. By being aware we cause the consciousness to wake up.

The big problem is that the consciousness is trapped in the subconscious and is small in proportion to the subconscious in the percentage of the psyche it forms.

When we are lost in a thought, a daydream, an ego, then we are in the subconscious (egos) and the consciousness is dormant. Most of the time is normally spent in the daydream of the mind and in subconscious states.

The consciousness trapped in that ego can be freed with the elimination of the particular ego that traps it. It then goes back to merge with the rest of the consciousness and that is how consciousness increases. As consciousness increases so does the capacity to be aware in daily life. There is a gradual waking up of consciousness, both in daily life and in dreams, because the level of consciousness here in the physical world is directly related to dreams. Without doing this work, consciousness normally constitutes about three percent of the whole psychological make up, while the egos (the subconscious) constitute the rest; so most activity takes place without being self-aware.

Therefore, for objective and clear Astral and dream experiences, the egos must be observed and eliminated and the consciousness increased. The less egos, the clearer the consciousness is and the clearer the experiences are. The more egos are present, the more the person sees their own projections of their subconscious.

On the Searching Within course, you will learn how consciousness functions and how you can activate it in your everyday life.

The Journey to Enlightenment course also explains how to transform the nature of the consciousness, to merge it with superior spiritual parts and how to advance along the spiritual Path. Consciousness is a tiny part of one larger Being, which is not present within a normal person but which exists in higher dimensions. It has many parts. To truly awaken spiritually, each of these parts needs to merge one by one with that basic essence.

This is a long and difficult process.

As the consciousness is merged with superior spiritual parts then true peace is found. A normal person can only feel the incipient peace emanating from the basic consciousness. True and profound peace is only possible when the spiritual parts of the Being are incarnated. Whoever has not done this will not know what it means.

The Different Parts of the Psyche in Different Planes

The different parts of the psyche reside in different planes. In the three-dimensional world while we are awake, we have the physical and Vital bodies, consciousness, thoughts, feelings and emotions, and a personality which we express ourselves through.

When we go into a higher dimension we leave behind the vehicles and faculties that are only needed for the lower dimensions. So when we go into dreams or consciously into the Astral plane, we leave behind the physical body in the third dimension and the Vital body in the fourth dimension. We are then there as consciousness, egos and personality.

In the three-dimensional world we can only see physical manifestations of the psyche; you can't see someone else's thought for example.

That's because the thoughts take place in the Mental plane of the fifth dimension and because the dimensions interpenetrate each other these thoughts have their effects on the physical body. This physical body is basically a vehicle for the other parts of the psyche to manifest in the physical world. Bodies are vehicles and I will say a little later about the bodies in the other dimensions.

Each dimension and plane from the third to the seventh

has less laws than the preceding one. That's why, for example, we can fly in the Astral plane - there are fewer laws constraining us. From the sixth dimension onwards we have the truly spiritual dimensions and planes where the lower aspects of the psyche cannot go. The infra-dimensions on the other hand, have more laws than the third dimension.

An ordinary person has, in the different dimensions the following:

Three-dimensional world: The physical body

Fourth dimension: The Vital or Etheric body

Fifth dimension, Astral plane: The Astral body (emotions)

Fifth dimension, Mental plane: The Mental body (thoughts)

Sixth dimension, Causal plane: The consciousness

Note that the Astral and Mental bodies are not true bodies in ordinary people. They are lunar phantom bodies that are basically just a covering of the egos. I'll say a little more about the true bodies later.

So when we sleep or Astral project or have any other out-of-body experience, we are leaving the physical body behind in the three-dimensional world (and leaving the Vital/Etheric body in the fourth dimension) while the parts of the psyche that belong to the dimension we go into and above, stay with us.

The Egos in the Fifth Dimension

When we go into the Astral plane we therefore have consciousness, personality and egos. These egos belong to two planes of the fifth dimension: the Astral and Mental planes. The Mental plane is higher than the Astral and has more freedom, but neither planes are exclusively spiritual as they contain egos and negative entities.

In the Astral plane, egos that give different feelings and emotions reside, while in the Mental plane, egos that give thoughts (negativity, pride, etc) reside.

The egos work from the Astral and Mental planes of the fifth dimension and manipulate the physical body. They then give rise to the different sensations in the psyche and in the body; they can make the heart beat faster, release adrenaline, produce trembling sensations, give rise to certain brain activity, etc.

Each of the different egos residing in the fifth dimension is a completely separate entity. They enter and leave the person, working through the fifth dimension to the third dimension according to the opportunity being available to them, and they take their food from the person's psychic energy. They enter the person one at a time in precise places in the psyche where, if we are observant, we can see them. When they leave, another ego comes in, which can then override or contradict previous ones.

Sometimes when falling asleep, particularly if trying to project, you can hear the noise when egos leave the physical body for the fifth dimension. This consists of moans, screams, shouts, babble and the like that are heard as though they are real sounds.

Children whose personalities are not yet fully formed, can sometimes see the different egos that have not yet been able to get into the child, usually before sleep at night. These appear as ghostly shapes and forms. They wait for the personality to be sufficiently mature before they can enter.

It is possible to investigate and see the different egos separately in the Mental plane. Through this you can discover much about how they work.

In the Astral they can appear as things separate to the person, in which case one may see something that looks like them doing an action of the ego, or incorporating into them, or the egos may appear symbolically as animals. Usually though, the person has them inside just as they do in the physical world, but mostly with less control as there is no physical world, which grounds one in forms of substance.

The egos also work to influence what is seen in the Astral and dreams, and create whole scenes and events that are no more than projections of the egos - a false world. If someone is awake and conscious in the Astral plane, freed from the projections of the egos and seeing the Astral as it actually is, they can see a dreamer looking like a drunken person; they can't seem to see properly, as though they have taken hallucinogenic drugs. If they are a little bit aware you might be able to get something through to them that they will remember when they wake up in the morning, but even then it is usually remembered through the person's own projections and self-created dream world. Only in times of clarity can objective Astral experiences be had. The person can even be projecting spiritual-like things that are no more than creations of their subconscious. That's why it is so important to study and understand the subconscious.

Negative entities can also use a person's egos to deceive the naive Astral traveler. Without working on the subconscious, a person has to rely upon occasional times when they have moments of clarity in their Astral experiences.

Dream or Astral experiences can sometimes be made clear, by the intervention of spiritual beings or one's own Being when someone needs to be taught, even though the psyche of that person may normally be very much dominated by their subconscious.

Anyone who is interested in understanding their psyche can learn a lot from remembering dreams and studying the different egos that they see in those dreams, as there they act freely without the restraints of the three-dimensional world.

The Personality in the Fifth Dimension

This is basically the vehicle through which consciousness and the egos manifest, so it goes into the fifth dimension with the rest of the psyche. With death it is left behind or when someone goes to a dimension above the fifth.

The Consciousness in the Sixth Dimension

If we are awake and consciously in the fifth dimension, the consciousness is present and active, but when dreaming it submerges into subconsciousness.

If, however, we go into the sixth dimension consciously, then we leave behind those things that belong to the lower dimension, so we are there with just the consciousness (this is a basic, simplistic description - the mind for example is quite complex).

As the sixth dimension is a dimension with no egos in it, it is the first of the truly spiritual dimensions.

Other Spiritual Parts in the Sixth and Seventh Dimensions

The consciousness is normally the only spiritual part that a person has, but there are other parts which are separate from it that never manifest within a person unless they have created a suitable body (vehicle) which they can manifest into.

Additionally, for a spiritual part to manifest within a body a person has to have a high degree of spiritual purity which is tested in the higher dimensions through the process of

Initiations.

These spiritual parts include Manas (in the Causal plane of the sixth dimension), Buddhi (in the Buddhic plane of the sixth dimension) and Atman or the Master (in the seventh dimension). There are other more spiritual parts than these too.

Bodies in the Higher Dimensions

A body is a vehicle that allows the psyche to manifest. The consciousness (the essential most fundamental part of every person) needs to be in the three-dimensional world so that it can awaken (more in the Journey to Enlightenment course). Through the evolution of life, the thoughts, emotions and personality allow that consciousness to function and interact in the three-dimensional world until it is mature enough to liberate itself from nature (to achieve enlightenment).

The bodies that a person is born with are a physical body, a Vital body, an Astral body and a Mental body.

Unfortunately, these bodies are very limited in what they can do; the Astral and Mental bodies are little more than a covering of the different subjective, subconscious components of the psyche (egos or selves). They do not allow for the manifestation of anything higher within a person than the basic consciousness or essence. They can be referred to as lunar bodies. They are phantom-like, not solid like a physical body is. The almost classic portrayal of a person projecting and looking like a ghost-like figure is the portrayal of a projection with a lunar body.

To be able to investigate properly and to function properly in both the higher and inferior dimensions a superior type of body is needed, one that is solid and allows for the proper rising of the Kundalini in it. That type of body is known as a Solar body; it has a radiance and is firm to the touch. It's not vague like a lunar body. These Solar bodies are the bridal garments referred to in early Christianity.

Now a body in the higher dimensions is not created by things like concentration, visualization, psychological observation, meditation, etc, but like all life it is born through sex - sexual Alchemy to be exact. Sex is the creative force; all energy is ultimately sexual. Whoever really wants to understand the mysteries of life has to understand the mysteries of sex.

So these Solar bodies can be created for the different dimensions. The lunar bodies become replaced with Solar ones and after that there are three new Solar bodies - two in the sixth (the Causal and Buddhic) and one in the seventh (the Atmic). These allow the manifestation of superior spiritual parts within the psyche, which ordinary people do not have and are part of the transformation of the psyche.

As some examples, the Solar Astral body allows the feeling of higher, more spiritual emotions. The Solar Mental body allows the capacity to instantaneously comprehend without the entanglements of the ordinary mind. The Solar body in the seventh dimension allows the manifestation of Atman, the Spirit, the Master. A few people are born with Solar Astral and Mental bodies that were created in past times, but most have lunar bodies and will need to create Solar ones if they want to do anything meaningfully spiritual and objective in the Astral plane. There are also higher bodies than the Solar ones: Golden bodies eventually with much work replace the Solar ones and allow for even higher spiritual parts to be incarnated. These Golden bodies in turn are finally replaced by bodies of Light. I have worked through this very difficult process on the Path and have Golden bodies.

107

Conclusion

When exploring the Astral plane, the psyche needs to be explored too. The Astral world and dreams cannot be taken in isolation as something separate from the study of self-knowledge. Indeed, the Astral world and self-knowledge cannot be taken as a complete study without including Alchemy and the esoteric Path, because it is the latter that is indispensable for profound and in-depth Astral experiences.

Week Four Exercises

Visualization/Concentration on a Place

This Week's Exercise

This week we are going to use the imagination and willpower to project to a place. The exercise is simple: when you go to sleep, visualize a place that you are familiar with.

When visualizing a place you need to picture it as realistically as you can. Visualize yourself walking in it so that it becomes concrete and real around you as though you were walking in a real place. Imagine that you can taste, touch, feel, smell, hear and see the things in that environment in an intense and real way. Learn to hear the sounds, smell the surroundings, feel the temperature and see things in detail. If you do this well enough you can be directly in that place, in that environment once the split from the physical body has taken place. Visualizing a place can also give you an instant insight into the place that you are visualizing.

If you try to visualize a fictitious place, which does not exist at all, you are going to create a fantasy, which will usually be nothing more than a projection of your own mind.

To project to a place you either consciously fly to that place in the Astral plane, or you just appear at that place in the Astral plane. Sometimes you travel to a place immediately, while other times you take time to get there.

Useful Tips When Astral Traveling to a Place

1. When you are flying to a place and encounter an obstacle, you should try to get out of it very gently. Avoid being confused by it; otherwise you are likely to be back in your physical body immediately.

2. Unless your intuition tells you otherwise, you should not get distracted with what you see while traveling, because you can get sidetracked and you may not make it to your destination. Many Astral traveling experiences come to an end in this way. You need to be disciplined when you are traveling and be very focused so that you get to your destination.

3. If you are flying at a very rapid speed, don't be afraid about it - just go along with it. If you try to slow down or stop it, you will probably be back in your physical body almost straight away.

4. Thoughts about your physical body or worries of how you are going to get back can end your Astral experience.

5. If you arrive at a place and you cannot see anything, you should use the conjurations taught later in the course.

6. If you are in the Astral plane and you can't see the place

you want to get to, visualize the place again and you will get closer to the place or you will land in the place.

A Point for a Better Visualization of Nature

If you visualize a place in nature, it will help your visualization if you go to a park or for a walk in the countryside and observe nature closer. Look at the trees, flowers, bushes, smell the aroma of flowers and nature. Also, listen to the different birds singing and try to remember them for your forest visualization. Try to observe the way clouds travel, the way birds fly, what happens when the wind blows, etc.

Exercise 1 - Astral Projection to a Room in Your House

This week's exercise is to try to project into a room in the house where you live. We will take a place that is real and familiar, because it will be simple to visualize to begin with - a room in the place that you live. The idea is that you visualize it and when you go to sleep, you go there in the Astral.

What you need to do is before you go to sleep, go into the room that you intend to project into and study it in great detail. Walk around and use all of your senses to perceive it. Look at all the objects, the different colors, the size of the room, the walls, the floor, etc. Be as aware as you possibly can be when you do this, not letting thoughts interrupt you. Take as long as you need to really take everything in and to feel present and aware in the place.

Go to sleep visualizing the room in great detail, perceiving it clearly, placing yourself back in it with your imagination, feeling that you are actually there, with the intention of

111

projecting there. If you do this well enough, you can rise out of your body or go to that place once the split from the physical body takes place. If you didn't manage to project, you could also find yourself waking up in a dream in the room, or going to the room. If you are a bit less successful, you could still dream about being in the room.

Of course, you don't need to stay in the room for the whole time that you are in the Astral plane; you can leave your room and travel.

For a variation on this exercise - if another person lives in the house with you who knows about the Astral, ask them to place an object in the room, an object that you know, but it should be put in a place that you do not know. Remember to study the object as well before you go to sleep. Go to sleep visualizing the room in great detail, placing yourself back in it with your imagination as before, but with the intention of projecting there and discovering where the object was placed. I did this exercise when I was first learning to project and was told that an object would be placed in the room we were visualizing. I projected and later, when back in the physical world, I spoke to the person who said he had put the object in the room (but he actually put nothing there) and I was able to accurately say to him that no object had been placed in the room.

Exercise 2 - Concentration/Visualization on a Place

During the day, to train yourself for the night exercise, choose any real place you have been to and visualize it for 10 minutes each day. Increase the time if you feel ready for it. You can also go into the room you are going to use for your night projection, then sit or lie down and visualize it.

Summary of This Week's Exercises

1. Astral Projection

Visualize your room at night as you go to sleep and project there.

2. Concentration/Visualization

During the day, visualize a place. Start with 10 minutes and increase it gradually if you feel able to.

3. Remembering Dreams

For this week, give more emphasis to remembering your dreams. The mantra is Raom Gaom.

Week 5

Waking Up in the Astral Plane From Dreams

*I*n this topic we are going to look at a simple technique through which you can become conscious in the Astral plane by waking up in a dream. With it, you can carry out exactly the same investigations in the Astral as you would do when you project from your bed.

In the normal course of sleep, dreams occur in the Astral plane, so it is possible to become conscious of being there while in a dream. It happens to many people and is commonly called 'lucid dreaming'.

However, there is a difference between a dream and being conscious in the Astral. When dreaming there is no recognition of being in a dream; it just happens and there is no self-awareness to enable us to realize where we are. When you are conscious in a dream however, you know that you are in a dream and then you are conscious in the Astral. This is why we use the term 'waking up in dreams' rather than 'lucid dreaming'.

There are exercises that can be done to become conscious in the Astral while dreaming. They basically involve questioning during the day to see whether you are in the Astral or in the physical world, in order to record that question in the subconscious and to repeat it while dreaming, and thereby to realize that you are there.

The things that are done during the day naturally become recorded in the subconscious. The subconscious then projects what it has recorded onto the Astral, which combines with what's actually there and becomes the scenes that form the dreams. In most cases, they seem real to the dreamer, but they are mostly just the dreamer's own creation. Yet everything that exists here actually has its counterpart in the Astral. Every physical form has its Astral form because things are multidimensional. So if we were awake in that dimension, we could see our house, town, friends, etc, but in a dream it is mostly altered. Even when we do wake up in the Astral, you can often see what is there, but occasionally the dream images continue due to the projections of the subconscious.

Reality Checks

During the day, if you make reality checks by repeatedly asking yourself where you are and whether you are in the physical world or in the Astral, that questioning gets eventually recorded in the subconscious and you will eventually ask that question at night while in a dream. Then, in the dream, you can realize that you are in the fifth dimension.

That dimension has different laws than here; we can fly and move through objects. So if we question ourselves here using things that only occur in the fifth dimension, for example flying, then we know what dimension we are in if they happen.

There are various things you could do to check where you are, but two that have proven to be very successful are jumping and pulling your finger. The first involves jumping slightly into the air, with the serious intention of floating or flying. Obviously, we're not going to fly here, but if we do it in the Astral then we will fly. If you do that enough here, you will begin to do it in dreams. Then when you jump and you actually float or fly, you can easily realize where you are and become conscious in the Astral.

When you practice this you don't need to jump very high, just slightly, but you do need to seriously question where you are and whether you are in the physical world or in the Astral. It is important to do this questioning sincerely, really asking yourself the question. If you do it and you think that you are really in the physical world, you will jump in the dream but you will think that you're in the physical and it won't work; you may just land straight back down or may fly convinced that you are in the physical. You also need to really do it with the feeling that you're going to fly. When you have flown a few times in the Astral you know how that feels.

The second check you can make is to question and to pull your finger at the same time. In the Astral, matter is different, so if we pull our finger there it stretches.

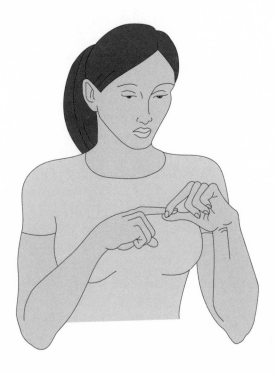

This is useful when it is inappropriate to jump in the air no matter how discreetly, and we want to check where we are (you don't want to look like an idiot bounding around the office for example).

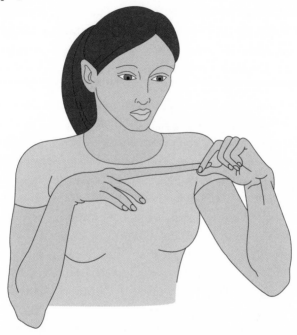

To make all this questioning work, it's important to do it very frequently, to be checking often during the day. Eventually this will become recorded in your subconscious and you will start to do it in your dreams.

When you question, it's best to do it with awareness, looking around carefully at the place you are in, the objects around you, etc.

You need to genuinely question where you are, actually doubting and wondering; if you don't, when you question in the dream, you can be convinced that you're in the physical world. Even to the extent of jumping up into the air, floating and wondering how you could float in the physical world, or thinking that you can float in the physical world. This has happened to me and to many students very often.

I used things to trigger off the remembrance of jumping by jumping whenever I saw certain things, knowing that whenever I saw those things in a dream I would be likely to question where I was and to jump. I used to help myself to remember to jump by jumping every time I saw the stars at night, then I would often be helped to wake up by being shown the night sky in a dream. Whatever you use to check, do it safely. Don't abandon safe behavior in order to check for the Astral plane.

Strange things that you see sometimes can also be used to remind you to question where you are because strange things happen very often in dreams. You might be looking into the night sky and see UFOs flying around for example. Whenever you see something strange or unusual, then use it to question whether you're in the physical world or in the Astral world. Then either pull your finger or jump to check.

Once, in a dream, I saw a spiritual Master called Rabolu in front of me and he jumped up in the air doing somersaults. I thought that it just couldn't happen and realized that I was in the Astral. In fact, I woke up in the Mental plane, which is a higher plane than the Astral, but still in the fifth dimension.

I have been in the Astral on different occasions and have met students who were in a dream. I remember asking one to wake up and jump; I told him that he was in the Astral, but he could only partially recognize me because of the dream images that he had. I jumped and floated but it made no difference, he was too asleep on that occasion, but he may have remembered seeing me in a dream if he had done the exercise to remember dreams when he woke up in the morning.

When a person dreams, they can look like people who we

see here drunk or on drugs to someone who is awake in the
Astral.

The Five Steps to Reality Checking

There are five main areas that need to be covered when
trying to successfully record the questioning of which dimension
you are in:

1. The Framework - This is the overall plan you have of
your Astral/esoteric work. To be really successful your esoteric
search needs to be the most important part of your life. Not just
as an idea, but in what you actually do. This will be made clearer
in the later Journey to Enlightenment course. What is important
is that during daily life, your mind is focused upon your inner
search and its related activities – so plan it out and carry out
your plan. However, working with the three key components
of the esoteric Path is the best way to create the framework.

The framework provides the direction so that the mind can
remember to question more often. At this stage, try to make
every day an opportunity to explore the Astral plane and base
your daily activities around it whenever you can, with your
daily Astral exercises, awareness walks, nightly projections, etc.
Group activities, such as those found in our study centers help
a lot too, and can enable you to focus more upon your inner
work.

2. Reminders - The framework you establish will play a
large part in you remembering to question where you are. The
more you are thinking about your esoteric exercises the more
you tend to remember to do them. So a large part in getting this
questioning recorded in the subconscious is acquiring the ability
to remember to question where you are in the first place.

Besides the framework, many people find it effective to set reminders that trigger off the questioning. I mentioned one that I found effective earlier when I used the stars at night to remind me to jump. Besides ordinary things, you could also make use of anything strange you might see in the physical dimension to remind you to question which dimension you are in.

Many people have found that setting reminders that catch the attention when doing other things also helps. For example, some people leave notes around their house reminding them to make a reality check, or set an alarm clock to go off at regular intervals, or when working on a computer to have something reminding them to question appearing every now and then. After a while though, it is easy to start ignoring or not bothering to put these mechanical reminders, so persistence will be needed if you choose to use them.

Another aid to remembering to question is to set a target for the number of reality checks to be made during the day - say 50 or 100 and then to try to meet that target.

When the framework created with the three key components is in place you may have all you need to remember to question, without needing other reminders, but having the reminders there as an option can be a useful way to get the questioning going again if it falls off a bit.

3. Question - It's the question and the following check that are the things that will actually record in the subconscious. The question should bring about that feeling of really wondering "Where am I?".

The question itself can be anything that will bring about that feeling and get you to check. So for example, you could ask whether you are in the physical dimension or in the Astral plane, or wonder how you got to the place you are in right now, whether there is anything strange happening around you, when you last went to sleep, asking what place you are in, etc.

4. Check - This is where you do something to see which dimension you are in, something that you cannot do in the third dimension, but can do in the fifth.

I have found it most effective to do physical rather than mental checks, such as jumping or pulling the finger as I described above. Anything safe that provides a physical check will work. I have tried slowly putting my hand through an object while in the Astral plane. But on one occasion I couldn't get it to go through the object and I didn't know where I was. Had I made a second check using something else such as pulling my finger, I would probably have confirmed that I was in the Astral plane.

5. Continue - Keep your inner esoteric work going after you have made the check. If you know about the self-observation as taught on the Searching Within course, continue with that. If you know about being aware, do it. Get your mind into the mode of practicing for the esoteric work. It will help the ability to remember to make your next reality check.

The Importance of Awareness

Awareness makes the consciousness (the essential you) active. The clearer that your level of consciousness in daily life is, the clearer and more lucid the dreams you have.

Awareness in dreams makes it easier to see what is going on in dreams and thereby makes it easier to remember to question where you are. So you can make better use of the opportunities to wake up there.

The consciousness can not only be activated, but also the amount of consciousness can be increased, which is very important. To increase the amount of consciousness you have, you will need to learn the techniques in the Searching Within and Journey to Enlightenment courses. These techniques involve Alchemy, which gives lucidity to the consciousness, and techniques to see and eliminate subconscious states such as fear, anger, various mental images, etc, which we call egos and which make up the subconscious. These keep each person in a daydream throughout daily life and that daydream continues when sleep arrives and becomes dreams. In this esoteric work on another course, you learn to eliminate those subconscious elements and to increase the amount of consciousness.

For now however, try to see what it is to be aware. Being aware exercises and feeds the consciousness that you have; it's a matter of getting out of the daydream and 'waking up' to where you are and the inner state that you have, in the present moment. If you catch yourself daydreaming go back to what you are doing immediately so that you cause the consciousness to wake up.

The more you can practice being aware of where you are, what your inner state is and what you are doing, the better. Combine this with questioning which dimension you are in and you have a very effective means of getting to the Astral plane.

Some Experiments and Exercises With Awareness

To get started with discovering how the awareness of the present moment works, try exercising it using these three activities. These are things that you are likely to be doing each day, but usually without being fully aware that you are doing them. The object of this exercise is to do these routine, mundane activities aware that you are doing them throughout as much of the time that you are doing them as you can.

The three activities are:
1. Washing yourself
2. Putting your shoes on and taking them off
3. Eating

So try to concentrate upon each of these activities when you do them, being aware of doing them and not allowing the mind to interfere and to take you off daydreaming. If you go off into a daydream, go straight back to the activity you are doing. Investigate how awareness works.

Discovering how awareness works is a matter for experimentation. Eventually an esotericist will aim to be aware and in self-observation throughout the whole day. This can be difficult to try to do, but to help get started, concentrate upon three activities that you do each day, start with these three, but later, change them around; making the effort to use them to practice being aware of what you're doing. Any activity can be used, but try these three. However well or difficult other things are going during the day, use these three activities to anchor yourself in awareness and self-observation. Then apply it throughout the day whenever you can remember to.

If you know about self-observation as taught on the Searching Within course, then apply it, because awareness should be done with it and is really part of it.

Also try awareness walks, where you go for a walk each day if you can, with the intention of being aware, observing yourself, and, at intervals, performing reality checks to question whether you are in the physical world or the Astral. If you walk to work or anywhere on a daily basis, you could also make it an awareness walk and incorporate it into your daily framework of esoteric activities.

Questions & Answers

Q. How do you know the difference between getting into the Astral plane by Astral projecting or by waking up in a dream?

A. The difference is only in the way that you get into the Astral plane. You can be in the same place from both methods; it is only the way that you get there that's different. With projection, you go straight into the Astral plane from the physical body (which you leave behind). When you wake up in a dream, you have missed the projection, but are still consciously in the Astral plane.

I'm not sure if this was Astral projection. At first when I went to sleep at about midnight or so, I was dreaming already, then I realized I was lucid dreaming. Then, when I kept on trying to get out of my body, I started feeling pains - in my dream. Then I lost that and I started dreaming again. This time I was lying down in bed trying to project because I knew I was dreaming.

Suddenly, I popped out of my body and I was just floating in the air in some brightly lit sky somewhere. I tried to will myself to go into my sister's bedroom. However, it felt like I was being pulled there and the candles in her room allowed me to see her dresser. After

that brief pull, I was pulled outside of my house and it was just me and the night sky. Then I suddenly found myself in my body again at 12:30 a.m.

Please tell me if this was Astral projection. I'm so positive that it is because I've never experienced anything like this before. Partly I doubt my experience as being a projection because I didn't get to have what people call spherical vision. Maybe that comes with practice. I've been thinking about it all day so any feedback is appreciated.

Yes, you were in the Astral plane. When you get pulled to a place like that it is generally because you need to be shown or experience something there. When a Master is called in the Astral there is also that pull (experienced by the Master).

Forget about having spherical vision or trying to perceive in a certain way, because that can make you create things from your own imagination that are not really there and make you lose the Astral, turning it into a dream or bringing you back to the body. It just becomes a distraction; it is best to be simple and clear in the Astral.

There are different faculties and senses that enable us to perceive what we cannot see with the eyes, but you really need to develop them here in the physical world.

Just try to be aware while you are there. Then any faculties will be naturally activated.

In the Astral, whatever you want to happen happens, I think, but I'm not a hundred percent sure about that.

It is not the case that whatever you want to happen happens. You can however imagine things in the Astral and they will appear. They don't really exist there though, they are projections of the mind and with them you can soon fall into a dream and lose awareness of the Astral. It is better to be clear of those projections so that we can actually see what is there.

127

I read about the ability to become anything, like a room or a flame or a chair. Do these things happen in the Astral, or is that something else?

You can imagine things in the Astral and they become real, but it is not advisable because then you don't see things as they are and you can miss out on teachings.

How much practicing did you do before you finally did it? I can't seem to get there with these exercises. I have projected before but it happened accidentally. I am starting to think that I am doing something wrong. Is it because I am too tired when I do try?

I had been developing awareness for six months before I tried Astral projection. I didn't know about the Astral before then, but because of all that training in awareness I managed to project first time.

So far, we have given just one basic exercise of projection, but there are more. It can take a lot of practice, time and patience to do the things necessary to achieve the Astral.

Try doing the 'jumping' exercise and pulling your finger during the day to get yourself to wake up in a dream. It is a very simple and effective exercise. If you are too tired, you can have difficulties projecting; the mind finds it difficult to focus then and sleep arrives so quickly. The remedy is to conserve your energies by being less in the egos during the day and to go to bed when you are not so tired.

In my experience, I tend to wake up from dreams either before the split or after. Is it normal to have dreams before the split?

You can have dream images before the split. You are getting into the Astral but are missing the process of projection.

Opening my eyes ended two of my experiences in the Astral. Should I not do this in future?

Yes, you can open your eyes without losing the Astral, but try not to be absorbed in what you see. You should watch your egos in the Astral because feeling nervous and the like can bring you back to your body.

I think I did it! When I was dreaming I suddenly thought, "Am I dreaming?" and realized that I was. Then I felt suddenly happy and free like I do when I am trying the awareness exercises in the daytime. However, as soon as I realized it my body started to feel fuzzy and vibrating and the place where I was dreaming disappeared and I felt as if I was waking up. I panicked because I thought I was seeing my room and my eyes were opening, so I told myself to keep in the dream, but then I must have fallen asleep again. Was this waking up in dreams? Why did I then wake up properly and how can I stop this?

Yes, you did wake up in a dream. It often only lasts for a short time as it did for you. Then you wake back up in the physical world or lose self-awareness in the Astral and merge back into a dream. This is usually due to a lack of awareness and consciousness, although heightened emotional states such as panic can also bring you back to the body. It helps if you can hold on to Astral matter while you are there and to stay as naturally aware as possible, eliminating any egos (emotional states for example) that arise.

I woke up in my dream and I thought, "Hey, this is a dream, now I should be able to do whatever I want." So I

tried, but nothing happened. Is it possible that I didn't actually wake up but just dreamt that I did and that's why I couldn't do what I wanted, or is there something you have to do before you can actually do what you want or Astral project?

You did wake in your dreams, but the idea you have about Astral projection threw it out.

What you really need to do and should have done is investigate that plane and seek knowledge there. If you improve internally and become more conscious, then you can learn things that you can't even imagine at this moment because the mind is a basic tool in comparison with what you can know through consciousness. Otherwise, you will be wasting your time there.

If you wake in your dreams again, try finding out how that dimension works. For example, what happens if you jump? Are things really as solid as they are in the physical plane? Then try to push through something that is solid and you will see for yourself what happens. Learn to investigate things; then you will discover much more.

I knew I wasn't in the Astral, but I thought that lucid dreams were where you could make anything happen. When I did jump in the dream I started to fly and then I woke up.

Lucid dreaming is an unclear term. When you know you are in a dream then it is an experience that is taking place in the Astral plane. Don't waste the opportunity by trying to make things happen, you will only see what is in your subconscious if you do. Rather, be aware of what is there - it will help you to stay out longer too.

A week ago, I was driving when I saw something strange and for a split second, I thought I was dreaming.

That night while dreaming I was driving and again saw something strange (a distortion of the windscreen). I thought that if I could concentrate on the distortion, I would see what was really there. At this point I realized I was in the Astral, but it was short lived. As I was driving in the dream when I woke, I thought I may have been driving in reality and nodded off at the wheel, so I panicked to find my body to make sure it was still okay - whoosh! back in my body, which of course was sleeping in bed. At least it is a start.

Yes, that is a good start. Don't forget to pull your finger and jump in the day. This will increase the chances of waking up in the Astral.

Lately I have tried to be more aware in my everyday life, focusing on seeing things in the present time rather than thoughts or emotions. Doing this I have realized I am remembering more of my dreams when I sleep and I am seeing more déjà vu scenarios of dreams or places I felt I have been before.

One night about a week and a half ago, towards the early hours in the morning (still dark outside), I felt I woke up within my dream state. This was quite unusual, but what made it more unusual was that as I woke within my dream. I could see a dark shape of something that I can't really specify, but it was about 20 cm in height and 5 cm in width and there was a number of different rainbow-like colors outside of the darker shape.

In this state of mind, while I was sleeping, I felt this was the stage for me to try to Astral travel so I tried to leave my body. As soon as I tried I snapped back into my body and was wide awake. I later learned I probably should not have willed my self out of my body, but let things take

place by themselves.

I would like to know whether this sounds like the right process for Astral travel or was I in dreamland seeing things? If that was a complete and utter load of nonsense, could someone explain to me what might have happened?

By waking up within a dream state, you were already in the Astral. There is no need to try to leave the body if you become self-aware in a dream. You should have tried jumping to make sure you were there.

If you see anything strange like that object again, use the conjurations, which will be given later in the course. Then you will be able to get rid of any kind of negative influence or entity and will (along with your intuition) be able to tell if something is good or is negative.

If you have just gone into the Astral, don't try to will yourself out of your body - actually get up slowly. As it was, you were just pulled back into it.

On the first day of the exercise, I asked myself a bunch of times if I was in the Astral or physical world. Last night I woke up, and decided to try to project again, which I do every night. This time I did project, but instead of walking outside of my house, it was a house in the country. I thought that I must be in a dream, but conscious. So I started walking when I realized something like a magnetic force was pulling me towards something. A policewoman told me which way to go and pointed. It was not necessary for her to do this as I was already going in that direction.

I came upon three or four people as I was floating by and asked where I was going. They said, "Toward and through the crosses." I said thanks and proceeded to go

further, but I woke up.

My question is, was this a test for me to try and accomplish or is this something I need to figure out on my own since it was in the dream part of the Astral?

It was an experience in which you were being taught.

When you are being pulled with a magnetic force like that it usually indicates that you are being led to a certain place. The policemen usually represent agents of the divine law (who are associated with Karma), just as the physical ones here are agents of a country's law here.

If the crosses were like graves, they could mean death, but the cross has a meaning - the responsibility and sacrifice of the esoteric work, and also the Alchemy.

You need to look at the particular experience and see what it means overall.

What role does the cosmic fire play in the Astral jump? Do I have to use it or is there no need to use the cosmic fire? I'm really concerned about how dangerous it can be.

There are many kinds of cosmic fire. The one we mostly refer to is called the Kundalini. It has to be awakened first with the true esoteric work, although many mistakenly think it's easy and give wrong techniques to try to awaken it. Once it has been awakened, there is no danger from it.

You will do best to continue trying the Astral at this stage and not to worry about the cosmic fire. That will be explained on the Journey to Enlightenment course.

I have had a couple of experiences where I was in a normal dream, all of a sudden noticed something really out of the normal and suddenly realized, "Hey, I'm dreaming." However, after this, I quickly lost control of the scene, and rather than being able to look at the images,

it all became swirled together, and then I woke up.

Is this control something that happens with practice, or should I be doing something else to keep from losing the images and waking up? I am discovering with the exercises of awareness during the day that I am remembering more of the dreams that I do have during the night and I am continuing to do the finger pulling/ jumping exercises.

It is a very common experience. What you need to watch is that you don't get too excited when you get into the Astral. If you keep working upon your emotions during the day, you will find in the future that the experiences will be clearer. Just keep persisting with it - you are on the right track. Keep learning and you will see that you are able to stay in the Astral for longer.

I was finally able to wake up in a dream after a day of relaxation exercises. I practiced the relaxation exercise and after a while, I fell asleep. When I woke up, I found myself in a city (I don't know where). I knew I was in a dream so I walked a few meters and I jumped with the will of flying and flew into the sky. A second after, I noticed a black bird that I passed and then fear arose in my whole body (although I'm not afraid of black birds in the physical plane). I hastily returned to my body by thinking and moving my body parts. I noticed that the time in my dream was the same in the physical but only advanced a little.

It's very important to overcome the fear. This is done by gaining experience in the Astral, by learning to use the conjurations and by doing the esoteric work here, which includes the elimination of ego states such as fear and Alchemy, which transforms the energies. You get fear when the energies are weak, but it goes away when they are strong. When you get the information on the conjurations later in this course and you see anything like that which makes you afraid again, you can conjure it to make it go away. Then you will get the confidence that you can deal with things in the Astral plane.

Yes, it is true that time is different there than it is here, because there we are in eternity when we are in the fifth dimension. But whenever you are shown the time in the Astral, you need to pay careful attention to it because the numbers of the time will give you an indication of how you are doing spiritually (there will also be more about this in another topic).

Week Five Exercises

Waking Up in the Astral Plane from Dreams

This Week's Exercise

This week we are going to concentrate fully on getting into the Astral plane from the dream state. This means that during this week you will need to work during the day and at night to get into the Astral plane.

This week you have an extra opportunity to experience the Astral world. If you do not manage to Astral project from your bed, you have a second chance to experience the Astral by waking in your dreams through the techniques you have been taught this week.

Here is a summary of the exercise:

Waking Up from Dreams

Practice the techniques of questioning, jumping and pulling your finger as much as you can during the day. For the effectiveness of this technique, read this week's topic carefully so that you have a really good idea of how to do it. It is important that you are genuine in your questioning and jumping.

Summary of This Week's Other Exercises

1. Awareness
Practice awareness during the day as explained in the topic.

2. Concentration/Visualization
Practice concentration/visualization on the heart for 10 minutes, but if you feel confident, you can increase it to 15 or 20 minutes.

3. Astral Projection
Practice Astral projection with the techniques of concentration/visualization on the heart.

4. Remembering Dreams
Practice remembering your dreams. You could have woken up in your dreams, but the heavy sleep could have wiped your memory of it. It will be worth your while to put a bit more work into remembering your dreams this week.

Week 6

Mantras for Astral Projection

*F*or this session we are going to study another technique for Astral projection, as concentration and visualization are not the only ways to Astral project. It is also possible to project using mantras, although you will still need to concentrate upon the mantra.

Mantras are constantly repeated sounds, words or phrases. They can be used for a variety of purposes such as increasing intuition or for remembering dreams, etc. For this topic I will mention mantras that are effective for Astral projection.

Three of the ones used here have an elongated pronunciation of vowels. Pronouncing the vowels like this stimulates the different Chakras in the Astral body. Chakras are senses of the Astral body. There are seven of them and each, when stimulated, give their own different psychic effects. In this case, they help the detachment of the connections that exist between the physical and Astral bodies.

It's worth remembering though that this pronouncing of mantras stimulates the Chakras and helps the projection just for the time that you do it. If you don't pronounce the mantras you are not going to get their benefits. However, when you do the spiritual work you can activate the Chakras and their corresponding faculties fully and permanently.

Pronouncing the Mantras

So for Astral projection we are going to use the following mantras and I am going to explain how to pronounce each of them. Have a listen to the sound files if you have access to them so that you can hear the mantras pronounced and will be able to pronounce them properly.

La Ra S - pronounced Laaaaaaaaaaa Rrraaaaaaaaaaa Sssssssssssssssss.
La - The vowel 'a' is pronounced as the 'a' in the word 'far'.
Ra - The 'r' is trilled. The 'a' is pronounced as the 'a' in the word 'far'.
S - The 's' is pronounced as the 's' in snake, like a hiss.
Breathe in through the nose; breathe out slowly through the mouth pronouncing the syllable.

You use one breath for each of the syllables. For example: (breath) Laaaaaaaaaaa, (breath) Rrraaaaaaaaaaa, (breath) Sssssssssssssssss.

Egypto - pronounced, Eeeeeeeeeeee hiiiiiiiiiiiiiip toooooooooooo.
E - The vowel 'e' is pronounced as the 'e' in the word let.

Hip - The vowel 'i' is pronounced as the 'ea' in the word tea, or the 'ee' in the word sheep.

To - The vowel 'o' is pronounced as the 'o' in the word more.

Breathe in through the nose; breathe out slowly through the mouth pronouncing the syllable.

You use one breath for each of the syllables. For example: (breath) Eeeeeeeeeeeeee, (breath) Hiiiiiiiiiiiiiip, (breath) Tooooooooooooo.

Fa Ra On - pronounced Faaaaaaaaaaaa Rrraaaaaaaaaaaa Ooooooooooonnnn.

Fa - The vowel 'a' is pronounced as the 'a' in the word 'far'.

Ra - The 'r' is trilled. The vowel 'a' is pronounced as the 'a' in the word 'far'.

On - The vowel 'o' is pronounced as the 'o' in the word more.

Breathe in through the nose; breathe out slowly through the mouth pronouncing the syllable.

You use one breath for each of the syllables. For example: (breath) Faaaaaaaaaaaaa, (breath) Rrraaaaaaaaaaaa, (breath) Ooooooooooonnnn.

You can practice a variation of this mantra by visualizing the Egyptian Pyramids while you do it. One example of this mantra working is a student of this course who pronounced this mantra and woke up in the Astral inside one of the Pyramids.

Tai Re Re Re Re – This mantra is different to the three previous ones.

Tai - pronounced as in the word 'Thai' (the inhabitants of

Thailand).

Re - pronounced as in the word 'rep' (short for 'representative', as in 'sales rep').

It is pronounced quickly, without elongating the vowels. Tai is pronounced once, and then you pronounce the other five syllables one after the other very quickly.

This mantra has a light singing tone to it. If you have access to them, listen to the sound files to get the tone of the mantra right.

This is all done in one breath and you continue repeating the whole mantra with each breath.

Pronounce these mantras until you Astral project or fall asleep. When you're pronouncing these mantras you still need to concentrate on them; they will be far less effective if you don't.

There are other mantras that can be used for Astral projection; you will come across those later, if you continue with the courses. These will be enough to be getting on with for a while.

You can listen to the mp3 sound files of the mantras by typing the following addresses into your Internet browser window:

http://www.gnosticweb.com/astralbook/La_Ra_S.mp3
http://www.gnosticweb.com/astralbook/Egypto.mp3
http://www.gnosticweb.com/astralbook/Fa_Ra_On.mp3
http://www.gnosticweb.com/astralbook/Tae_Re_Re.mp3

Projecting With the Mantras

It's best to develop a certain mantra (such as Fa Ra On for example) and try it for a few days in a row or longer, so that you allow the Chakras to activate more with the particular mantra, because some activate different Chakras than others. Bear in mind that you can practice the Astral at any time of the day; the morning can be a particularly good time. When you choose a mantra, stick with it for the duration of the exercise: don't change to another mantra or to a different type of exercise.

Concentration upon pronouncing the mantras is important, because if you don't have it you could lose track of the syllables you are pronouncing, because they are interrupted by thoughts. Then you can forget where you are in the mantra, the continuity of it will be broken and disrupted and the exercise will be weakened.

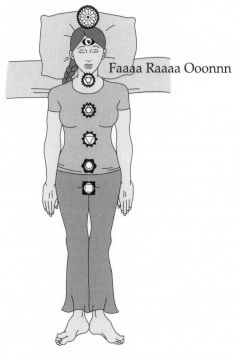

Faaaa Raaaa Ooonnn

Because these mantras work by stimulating the Chakras, you will increase their effectiveness by practicing the mantra you are going to use for projection for between 10 minutes and an hour at some time before you try to Astral project. This will get the Chakra spinning and partially activated, so that when you do your projection exercise you have the advantage of the activated Chakra, which will help the projection a great deal.

When you use these mantras to project with you need to be lying down ready to sleep, as you would when practicing concentration for Astral projection. Relax the body, then pronounce the mantra aloud for a short time, then get progressively quieter until you are only pronouncing it in your mind. From then on breathe as normal, as you no longer need to take a deep breath to pronounce the mantra aloud. Then continue pronouncing it over and over in your mind until sleep arrives.

If you cannot pronounce it aloud in the beginning for any reason, pronounce it mentally from the beginning.

The process of going into the Astral with mantras is the same as with concentration, with the electric like current and so on. However, parts of the Astral body may more noticeably begin to detach from the physical body; for example, an arm or a leg may lift up, or a hand or fingers may move, or your face may be in a different direction to the one you are lying in. When anything like this happens, you may not realize that the body has detached. I have known a student who was doing this exercise and was spinning around, wondering what was happening, but he didn't realize, or the thought never occurred to him that he was actually in the Astral. On the other hand, I have known of a student who realized this when pronouncing mantras and Astral projected 10 times in one night, repeating the mantra each time and getting up whenever a body part moved.

So if any of these things happen, or you have begun to float, and you think you might have projected, slowly get up from the bed (you need to do it gently or you can wake yourself up) or roll over out of bed gently and check whether you are in the Astral plane in the ways that I have mentioned in previous topics. If you are in the physical, go back to bed and try again; once the signs appear again, get up. If you keep doing this you will eventually get up in the Astral. However, you may also lift out of the body or wake up already in the Astral from pronouncing these mantras.

You need to train yourself to get up from bed when the parts of your body begin to move. Don't pretend or imagine that you are getting up; you have to actually get up from bed.

Like everything with Astral projection, a lot of patience is required and for some people it can take a long time. Nevertheless, if you persist you will find that it will eventually work.

Questions & Answers

Q. Part of the problem with the mantra is that I cannot pronounce it out loud. I think I will continue with the heart concentration exercise for now and wait for a few weeks until my wife is working nights for a week to try mantras.

In any one night does it matter if I swap around between the heart and a mantra i.e. go to sleep concentrating on the heart and then waking up later to try a mantra?

A. If you can't pronounce it out loud, but you still want to use a mantra for projection, just pronounce it mentally. It doesn't really matter if you swap around in one night between concentration and a mantra if you already have concentration, but it will help to develop your concentration and your ability to experience the exercise if you concentrate on one for a while, because then you can learn more about it. Not only that, but because the mantras activate the Chakras, continuity will allow them to maintain a standard. If you change to another exercise for one or more nights, the Chakras may be less sensitive. Continuity is usually important in developing any Astral exercise.

In my home office I have a comfortable armchair giving support to my back and neck. Is it possible to project while

sitting relaxed in a chair and concentrating on my heart during the day? Sometimes I will have opportunity to try this, but I just haven't bothered to date because I thought it wouldn't work.

You can project from any position as long as you can concentrate on the exercise and can sleep, although lying on the back is the position that most people find works best.

I tried the exercise in the afternoon by saying the mantra Tai Re Re Re and I felt really heavy, swirling movements and a sense of dizziness. This increased when I visualized my Astral legs moving, etc. However, I then got up and I was still in the physical, but I still felt the sensations quickly when I tried it again. Am I getting close and is it alright to visualize the body separating? Am I trying to get up too quickly? Should I leave it for a longer time?

You are getting close, but you shouldn't visualize the parts of the body moving. You just focus on the mantra and they can begin to move by themselves. Visualizing the body moving is part of the same problem; it distracts you from focusing on the mantra and can disrupt the exercise.

You are trying to get up too quickly: you should leave it for a longer time, until either the body parts begin to move of their own accord, or you begin floating upwards.

If there are three words in a mantra, do I sound each word in the same tone? Does it matter whether I do or not?

Yes, sound each word in the same tone. It will be evenly repetitive and will then work better.

In a previous lesson you said that if you stop practicing

the concentration exercise you would lose what you have built up very quickly. If I swap to using mantras for the next week or so, will I loose what I have built up in concentrating on the heart? Should I alternate nights, or do they compliment each other?

It's just about alright because you are still concentrating on the mantra, but continue with the concentration/visualization exercises that are a preparation for the Astral. Try those at other times during the day and they will help to build up or maintain the concentration.

I have a lot of periods during day where I am free for 5-10 minutes (I can be sitting, but not lying down). Are there any simple exercises you can recommend that will help me improve my ability to Astral project?

You can do a basic concentration/visualization exercise that will keep your concentration going for the Astral. Take any of the concentration/visualization exercises on this course. For example, look at an object carefully, then close your eyes and recreate the image in great detail; when you lose it, open your eyes again and repeat the process.

Seeing that I share a bed with my wife and she is a light sleeper (don't think she will be too impressed if I wake her a few times a night getting up to see if I am in Astral), is there any less obtrusive way to check, i.e. pulling my finger when I am lying in bed? Also, I will not be able to say a mantra out loud, will this affect my ability to Astral project significantly?

You can try pulling your finger while you are still in bed to check and wait for sure signs of projecting before you try to get up in the Astral. It's only around the first seven times that you pronounce the mantra aloud, so saying it mentally still works - it's just a bit more difficult.

If you are doing a mantra exercise during the day, I assume you should keep your eyes closed. Would it be of benefit to wear an eye cover to block out light? Will concentration on the heart exercises work equally well in the daytime?

Most people find that just closing the eyes is fine, but there is no problem using an eye cover to block out the light if you feel that you need to use one. Concentration on the heart will work in the daytime. There are more mystical energies at night, but a projection exercise can work at any time.

I have heard that you should visualize Pyramids for Fa Ra On, but I am going to use La Ra S (I like the sound of it). Is there anything I should visualize for this one to make it more effective? When you say to concentrate on them, do you mean to concentrate on how they sound or the 'feelings' they invoke?

You don't have to visualize Pyramids for Fa Ra On, it's just an option. You can do La Ra S without visualizing anything. You concentrate on doing the mantras without thinking about how they sound or feel.

Can anyone tell me what it means to trill the 'R' in the mantra La Ra S? My first language is French, so does it mean to roll the 'R' as we do in French?

I think it would be like the French, but I don't know exactly how that is pronounced. The 'r' is trilled in many languages, although I am not familiar with most of them. I know that it's trilled in Welsh and in some Arabic languages. Just check with the sound files and you'll be able to tell.

Every night, I practice the mantra Fa Ra On until falling asleep, but I find it difficult to project with mantras. I am

not used to it but I will get used to it and practice the techniques given in these courses. I just hope it will work some day.

If you persist you can find that it eventually works, but everything takes practice to achieve. As an alternative with the mantra Fa Ra On, pronounce it while visualizing the Pyramids, as real as you can. Look at a picture of the Pyramids beforehand if you think it will help.

The physical pronouncing of the mantra aloud shouldn't go for long or you may not attract sleep. When you are doing a mantra internally, do it softly, so that you attract sleep.

I was just wondering, when I projected before I had my vision and my head was out, but when the feet and hands came out, everything was dark as though my eyes were still closed. If I were to have gotten up at this point, what would have happened? Would I have had my sight? It felt like the bottom half of my body was out and the top half was still in the physical. Is that possible?

If you got up at that point, you could have projected, even though it was dark, because the bodies were already separating. It may or may not still be dark often depending on your state.

If you get into the Astral and it's dark, you can use something to clear it called a conjuration, which I will explain about later on this course.

I have found that when I do any of the concentration practices in order to project, after a while I get absolutely freezing feet! I never experience cold feet at any other time, except when I am practicing these Astral exercises and the longer I do the exercise for, the colder they get. It has got to the point where I have to wear ski socks every time I do a practice and my feet are still cold! Has anyone

else experienced this? Do you know why this might be?

Yes, the body gets colder as we fall asleep. We normally don't notice it, but if we try to Astral project, we go much further into the process of sleep and are aware of the increasing cold. Some may be more affected than others.

I don't have a clue if I'm saying the mantras at the right speed or tone.

The ones with elongated vowels are pronounced slowly for as long as each breath lasts; listen to the sound files carefully if you have access to them and practice the mantras with them.

Well I think I had my first experience, but I'm not sure. It scared me to death though. I was lying on my side saying the mantras aloud and as I felt more relaxed I started saying them mentally. The heartbeat was really noticeable too. Well, I felt myself trying to roll over and get up, but at the same time I was scared and yelling no and for someone to help me! It was like a force was pulling at me but the fear I felt was unbelievable. I even found myself trying to grab my hubby's arm beside me to keep from leaving my body. Then I woke up.

Was I almost there or was this something else? I have never experienced anything like this before. I was aware of everything during all this. Also, I read that once you have the ability to project, you can visit any place you want to go and even go see loved ones that live far away. Is this true?

Yes, you were there; you had split and were leaving your physical body. If you hadn't been so afraid you would have gone right out into the room in the Astral. You learn eventually that there is nothing to be afraid of; the fear of the unknown can be strong in the beginning. Fear generally is what we call an 'ego'. If you learn how to get rid of them, then this combined with Alchemy, (both in future courses) will gradually remove fear.

Once you are in the Astral, through whatever means, you can travel to most places.

I read through the article and exercise on the mantra Egypt. I have been doing it for one week now when I go to bed with only little results. That was until last night. As I was doing the mantra Egypt I fell asleep. Then I woke up and realized that I was separating from my body, and it seemed like I was in some sort of weird trance. I was conscious and was having trouble separating from my body. I was reaching, pulling on anything I could reach for, scared and confused. I forgot everything I was taught in the previous lessons about how to handle these situations.

The thing that scared me the most was that before my eyes a big teddy bear appeared sitting in my chair and turned and looked at me. This scared me so much that I screamed to myself to wake up. It took a little while but I eventually woke up scared. I was not scared because something threatened me - I was scared of the unknown, scared because it took me a while to come back to my body, scared because this was actually happening. After all that happened I told myself after I woke up that I will never try to Astral project again. Now after I thought about it, I realize this is a gift and I should use it. Tell me, how can I overcome my fear of the unknown?

There is a fear of the unknown that you can overcome with experience. Fear generally can be overcome with Alchemy and the elimination of those negative inner states (egos), both of which will be explained about in the Journey to Enlightenment course. This gives an inner strength.

The teddy bear may have shown you that in the state you were in, even the most harmless thing was causing you to be afraid.

Remember though, that negative forces use fear to stop any Astral investigation. If you give into them they will have won, but if you don't, you will find a whole new world opening up for you. The conjurations on this course will help to deal with them.

I've been using the mantras now every night since I got the lesson. The first night I felt like my foot twisted up and started to wiggle about, and I don't think it was my actual foot, as I didn't seem to feel any resistance from the bed covers. The second night I felt my thumb suddenly jump up as well. Then I felt the sensation in my feet disappear and this slowly worked its way up though my legs, then my hands and up my arms. Does all this sound normal? Am I on the right track?

I get an itching feeling on my face and other places like my back and neck, what is that? I try to refrain from scratching but it just gets too much and I can't focus on the heart when it happens.

Yes, it's normal and you are on the right track, but when your foot twisted up and your thumb suddenly jumped up, you should have slowly got up, because the bodies had already split.

Itching like that is very common in the beginning and is highlighted by an ego, a subconscious state. If you go back to concentrating on the exercise, it will reduce and go away. Then you find at future times it is not there or goes away easily. Ignore it. The body is trained with practice: you just keep going and eventually you will get there.

Week Six Exercises

Mantras for Astral Projection

This Week's Exercises

For the next two weeks we are going to try to Astral project with mantras. If you do them methodically each day for these two weeks, you will have a much better chance of succeeding than if you just try a mix of things here and there. Listen to the sound files carefully if you have access to the Internet. The pronunciation of mantras is important because the vowels in the mantras act on the many Chakras of the Astral body. This week you will also be spending some time pronouncing them well before you try to Astral project with them.

Exercise 1 - Mantras for Astral Projection

We will work with two mantras this week. The first mantra to try is La Ra S and then move on to the mantra Egypto. This will give the opportunity to develop each of them properly and to learn how each one works, because they are all different. If you keep to a particular one for long enough, you will activate that Chakra much more, making the exercise more effective.

It is also important that you find out at the end of these two weeks which mantra works best for you. There will be exercises in the future where you will need to choose the technique or the mantra you are going to work with in those exercises.

Two Important Points to Remember

1. Mantras should not be mixed. If you find a mantra is not working and you decide to change it for another one within an exercise, it will spoil your attempts to Astral project and your exercise will usually become mechanical without the needed focus. If you start an exercise with a particular mantra, train yourself to carry on with it to the end. In this way, you develop will power, learn to be consistent and to investigate things, finding out for yourself how they work.

2. When pronouncing mantras, try to be as focused and concentrated as you can be and do not allow thoughts to take you into a daydream.

Tips for Success with Mantras

1. When pronouncing mantras mentally, do not be tense and force them - it will keep you awake if you do. Relax and pronounce them gently. You are supposed to attract sleep while pronouncing them.

2. While pronouncing mantras mentally for a while, don't go along with initial thoughts that you cannot sleep simply because you feel you are awake or hear physical noise around you. It could be the case that you have already entered the transition period between wakefulness and sleep, which means that you could be very close to projecting. If that is the case you just need to keep going with your exercise.

3. If you feel that parts of your Astral body are moving by themselves, or if you feel that your physical body is asleep and you are somehow awake, it is time to get up. You should get up gently even if you think it is the physical world. Sometimes you may be surprised if you get up in the Astral world when you thought you were in the physical.

4. When you are getting up in the Astral plane and find that your feet get tangled in your sheets or in your bedding, gently get your feet out from them. Always be on guard not to wake yourself up physically while getting up.

5. If you manage to Astral project with a mantra and you come back to your physical body soon after, you can go back into the Astral again by pronouncing the same mantra again. The best thing is not to move once you have come back to the physical world. Stay in the same position, pronounce the mantra mentally again and take off. You will notice that the more you do it the more you know when to get up. You will reach a point where you won't need to decide when to get up - when the time is right you will learn to do it straight away.

6. Before you start your Astral projection exercise, you need to check within yourself that you really mean to Astral project and that you have the faith that you can do it. Likewise, once in the Astral you need to mean to go to places

and don't be hesitant by thinking that you may not be able to do it. Doubt is something that can really spoil your Astral exercises.

7. Finally, remember not to scratch an itch. If you do, the itch will appear somewhere else and your exercise may never start at all, or it may turn out to be a very shallow attempt. Learn to ignore an itch.

Exercise 2 - Vocalizing Mantras

As well as trying to project using mantras, try practicing them during the day by pronouncing them aloud.

You can start vocalizing a mantra for 20 minutes or more, rather than the 10-minute starting time for the concentration/ visualization exercises, but you should still build up gradually according to your capacity.

Vocalizing mantras for Astral projection is a good way to get ready for your exercise of Astral projection and to activate the Chakras. You could pronounce them lying down on your bed, on the floor, or seated comfortably somewhere.

The vocalization of mantras should be done at a different time to your Astral projection exercises. This will give you the chance to learn to pronounce them well and to find out what a mantra can do for you.

Summary of Exercises for This Week

1. Practice Astral Projection

The first exercise for this week is to try to Astral project with the mantra La Ra S for the first three days of the week, and then with the mantra Egypto for the next three days of the week.

2.   Vocalize a Mantra

Vocalize the mantra you will be trying for your Astral projection exercise that night, for 20 minutes or more each day, at a different time from your Astral projection exercise, and whenever is convenient for you.

3.   Waking up in Dreams

Use the technique of questioning, jumping and pulling your finger when you see there is something strange around you. Question yourself genuinely whether you are in the physical world or in the Astral world.

4.   Remembering Dreams

Remember your dreams either by not moving when you wake up or by pronouncing the mantra Raom Gaom.

5.   Optional Exercise of Visualization/Concentration

If you want to maintain or to continue improving your sharpness in your ability to concentrate, keep up your daily visualization exercises, using the techniques you have learnt on the course so far.

Week 7

DEALING WITH NEGATIVE ENTITIES

Negative Entities

*I*t's part of the structure of the way that life is created, that opposites exist. We have positive and negative, light and dark, etc.

This is necessary for life to exist; it is also necessary for learning and spiritual growth. If we had always existed in light alone, we would have no knowledge even of our own existence. It is the struggle against the darkness that makes us strong and gives us knowledge.

So we live here in this world, with all its duality and its opposites. But these opposites also exist in the fifth dimension, so negative things can be experienced in dreams or when consciously in the Astral plane.

Just as there are divine spiritual beings, so too there are beings who are the opposite - negative beings. The beings that are divine are that way because they have created themselves to be so. The same applies to the negative beings; they have transformed themselves into creatures of darkness. It is the aim of these esoteric studies to explain how to transform oneself into a Being of light, for which the darkness within (the egos, the different elements of the subconscious) must be overcome and the forces of darkness outside must be defeated in their attempt to stop one from awakening. They inevitably come to try to stop anyone who takes up the spiritual work.

These beings of darkness are the ones that you may have seen in nightmares or in dreams. They are the demons that are represented in the different religions throughout the world. Many people when Astral projecting have been met by them or have sensed their presence regardless of whether they had any religious convictions or not.

They belong to a hierarchical structure of evil beings, organized according to the level of awakened evil consciousness that each of them has. We find them in the Astral and Mental planes of the fifth dimension, although they reside in the inferior dimensions and enter the Astral and Mental planes.

They do not so much as cause harm physically as harm someone's spiritual development. For example, when you get to the Astral there may be some waiting there for you, to frighten you so that you fly back to your body, or to distract you so that you don't go somewhere more spiritual, or discover what you need to.

To the unwary they use deceit; they can say things that are misleading and can easily fool someone into taking their advice, which inevitably is harmful for the real spiritual work. They can even appear as ones idea of holy beings, preaching about love, etc, but their real purpose is to take us away from the true Path.

They can stir up egos, both in the Astral plane and in daily life, inflaming passions and desires and leading one astray. They can cause the Astral to look unclear or darkened. They can make an initiate fall and can do works on the Astral body so that the Kundalini, an essential aspect of the spiritual Path, does not rise, rendering the body useless for the esoteric work.

Not long after I had begun to practice all the key components needed to start the esoteric Path, I was giving lectures in a city when two new students joined; they were partners, but not married. They looked like two angels - young, with blonde hair - and impressed me with their ability to Astral project at will every night.

The woman had been in the national newspapers as many people had supposedly seen her flying over the top of a building. I was impressed, but I began to have doubts about the source of their powers. The way they had achieved their powers was not through the slow hard work that each of us must do, but had supposedly started after a car crash in which they should have died.

Doubts appeared too, when we left them in a room with a pentagram (this is a symbol that protects against evil forces when it is used the right way up). After they left the room, I noticed that the pentagram had been taken down and was placed the wrong way up.

One night in the Astral I saw the guy doing a work on my spine, where the Kundalini rises and inserting things into my kidneys that blocked the flow of energy. After this, a Master of the White Lodge called Rabolu appeared to me in the Astral and gave me a Century plant (more on this in a future course), which is used for protection. Then I asked the beings of light to undo what the negative beings had done to me. I conducted an exercise with a group of people (one that will be explained in a future course) to break their evil influence. I saw them both the next day and they looked completely different. Gone was the angelic look, instead they looked like a couple of vampires. Their faces were even swollen and they were only able to babble a load of rubbish.

We never saw them physically after that, although some months later I met the guy again in the Astral. This time however, I commanded him to reveal himself to me. He lifted into the air, turned into a grotesque demon and disappeared into the darkness from where he came.

These were two people who had awakened their consciousness for evil, but this time thanks to the protection of the Beings of light, they had failed in their evil mission.

This example is very unusual, because such beings are mostly found when we go to the Astral. Some of you on the course have already experienced a little of these negative entities from experiences in the Astral, and those of you who will go there in the future are very likely to meet them, even more so if you actually take up the spiritual work properly.

There are many cases in history and folklore of these beings. One very well recorded type of encounter happens when a person is partly in the Astral, lying in bed and feels totally paralyzed (this kind of paralysis is a function that prevents sleepwalking), sensing or seeing a negative entity close by or actually in contact with them. These entities can take advantage of that natural time when we're not quite in the physical body and not quite detached in the Astral and so are unable to move.

In times like this, as long as you are conscious, you can use what we call conjurations, which are words that dispel evil entities.

Conjurations

These are phrases that have the power to return negative entities back to their abode or to disable them. They have been used throughout history and references can be found in many esoteric texts. They work best when done strongly with a lot of conviction and when one's energies are strong.

Whenever you see an evil entity in the Astral, or a being that you are unsure of, or if you go into the Astral and it's dark, or in the physical world if you sense a negative vibe or presence, or before going to sleep, you should use them.

There are various formulas that have been recommended as conjurations. Two that I have used and found to be very effective are 'Jupiter' and 'Bellilin'. They are both available as sound files, which you can download from the website.

Jupiter

Jupiter is another name for the Christian 'Father'. To do this conjuration, you place your left hand over your Solar Plexus, which is around the navel. This protects against evil entities while the conjuration is being pronounced.

You put the fingers of your right hand in the shape of a gun with the index and middle fingers extended, the other two fingers closed and the thumb up. Extend your arm straight in front of you, pointing at the entity if you see one, and then pronounce the following words three times:

In the Name of Jupiter,
Father of Gods,
I conjure you,
Te Vigos Cosilim.

You say all that three times.

If you are in the Astral, you can sometimes see rays coming out of your hand, so you can imagine the rays as you do it in the physical world.

You can listen to the mp3 sound file of this conjuration by typing the following address into your Internet browser window:

http://www.gnosticweb.com/astralbook/Jupiter.mp3

Bellilin

You don't need to do anything with your arms with this one; you sing it, using the sound file as a guide to learn it.

Here are the words. You pronounce it three times:

Bellilin Bellilin Bellilin,
Amphora of salvation,
I would like to be next to you,
Materialism has no strength next to me,
Bellilin Bellilin Bellilin.

You can download an mp3 sound file of this conjuration by typing the following address into your Internet browser:

http://www.gnosticweb.com/astralbook/Bellilin.mp3

Bellilin is a divine wind that blows away negativity. This conjuration is particularly useful if for some reason you cannot move or cannot put your hands into position for the conjuration of Jupiter.

You need to say any conjuration all the way through three times for it to be fully effective.

There is no need to be frightened if the entity is still there while you are still pronouncing the conjuration, although it can sometimes disappear once you begin the conjuration. If it is there while you're doing it, continue and the conjuration will be effective as soon as you finish.

I remember a horrible animal attacking me in the Astral. As soon as I saw it I began to use Jupiter, because it's faster. It started running at me and bit me on the arm, even though I was conjuring it. I continued to conjure away and the animal stayed there, it only left when I had completed the conjuration totally.

If for any reason you come across something and you are not sure whether it is from the good side or from the evil side, use a conjuration to check. If it's good it will stay, if it's bad it will usually go or be disabled.

Many people have been deceived by these entities, so if in doubt, conjure away. But also use your intuition, because sometimes you can tell an evil entity just by looking at it, particularly if you look into its eyes, which can look dark and evil. Many times I have been met by an entity who took the form of a spiritual guide in order to deceive me, but you can learn to tell what they really are just by looking into their eyes. If you see that they are evil, conjure them so that they go away.

If you are negative towards someone, your own subconscious can make them appear as a negative entity to you in a dream or the Astral. In that case your own negativity may persuade you that it was real. This is another reason to work to get the psyche clear and objective.

In the Astral you can call spiritual beings and get help and teachings from them, but often if you call, a negative entity will arrive that looks exactly like the spiritual being you are calling, so use your intuition and conjure away if you need to. If the entity is evil it will go; if it is the real one, it will stay, and don't worry, the good ones don't get offended if you conjure them away.

You can also use the conjurations at night before you go to sleep, so that you clear away any negative entities that might be there or might appear during the night.

Circle of Protection

When the environment is cleared of negative entities with a conjuration, the area needs to be protected and sealed so that they, or others, cannot come back in straight away. For this, a protective circle is needed. This is a circle of light that is held by the elementals of nature, which forms a barrier that stops any evil entity from entering. It is drawn in a circle, using the imagination and doing a work with the elementals of nature, which makes the circle strong and sustains it.

Elementals of nature are essences (the raw consciousnesses) of creatures that are evolving. They have been known throughout history in various myths and legends as fairies, pixies, gnomes, salamanders, sylphs, etc.

They have been used by ancient peoples to protect sacred or important things. We hear tales, for example, of ancient burial grounds being protected by loads of snakes, or by swarms of bees.

An old depiction of a
Circle of Protection

Overlooking the town where I grew up is an ancient Britons (Welsh Celtic) burial site. Legends said that these sites were protected by bees and indeed there were very many recorded cases of people disrupting the sites and being attacked by bees. So when some unemployed people were made to work for their unemployment benefit by cutting steps into the burial site, they found that huge swarms of bees seemed to appear out of nowhere and covered their van.

Many ancient peoples knew how to work with these elementals of nature; they are the same ones that we use for this circle.

Having conjured away, then you draw the circle. It is done like this.

You say the following words:

My Father please, order my elemental intercessor to wrap a magical circle of protection around me (or the bed or the room or whatever you choose), *so that no evil entity can harm me.*

As you are saying the above you imagine a circle formed by a beam of light being drawn around wherever you have chosen.

The Father is the male aspect of each ones own Being. We ask that part of the Being because he has the power to do it.

You do this three times making sure that the circle is joined and complete.

This can be done before going to bed at night, or at any time that you feel you need to do it. Then once it's done, no evil entity can get in. The circle stays until you move out of it physically. When you move out of it physically, you break it.

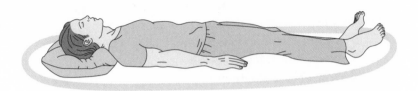

Some years ago a student of ours was a bit skeptical about this, but nevertheless he drew the circle around himself before going to sleep. He woke up in the Astral to find himself unable to move, with an evil looking cat in front of him. He became frightened and started spitting at the cat, because that was all he thought he could do. Then he noticed that he had a circle of light around him and that the cat could not get in. He then woke up, back in his body. He should have practiced the conjuration of Bellilin more because he could have used it to make the cat disappear.

Jesus used a circle of protection when he protected a woman who was about to be stoned. He drew a circle in the sand around her and she was saved.

The more that you practice these conjurations, the more you will remember to use them and remember the words to them in the Astral. You can also find yourself using them in your dreams if you practice them enough.

Once you actually use them, you see just how effective they are and you realize that you are able to deal with negative entities and are able to go and get teachings in the Astral plane unhindered by them.

So practice them and get them right, because you will need them.

Questions & Answers

Q. What does Amphora mean? Does it have a translation? Does it mean jug or container?

A. Yes, Amphora means a container, but one of a spiritual nature.

What does 'Te Vigos Cosilim' mean? Who is Bellilin? What does it mean?

They are both words that dispel evil that come from the higher dimensions. Te Vigos Cosilim doesn't have a literal translation here, although the Hindus used Bellilin to represent a wind that casts away evil.

Are there also other ways of dealing with negative entities besides the conjurations and circle? I have heard that if you mention Jesus's name these entities disappear.

Pronouncing a Master's name is not a reliable way of getting rid of them. You will find it more effective to use one of the conjurations on the course rather than using the name of a Master. Negative entities even often appear in disguise when you invoke a Master in the Astral.

Are some of these entities created by us from negative

habits like negative thinking or even smoking?

These entities are beings that have awakened in evil. However, there are entities that are created by people, called larvae. These predominate in places where there is a lot of emotion, where egos predominate, for example in a room where there has been a lot of anger, lust, or drunkenness. These larvae harm the Astral body.

There are also ones that are created by sexual desires, which are called incubus or succubus. They have an existence outside of the individual, and have to be destroyed with an Alchemical work, which is explained in the Journey to Enlightenment course.

There are also the parts of the subconscious that affect the Astral, which we call egos. These are various elements such as anger, pride, fear, etc.

When you dream about a negative creature, does that mean that in the Astral there is a negative entity that is working on you? I had a dream about a vampire bat and it flew down and bit me in the left shoulder. It felt so real and I couldn't get it off of me. I woke up and my shoulder felt funny. Was something doing me harm in the Astral and I just didn't realize I was in the Astral?

Yes, it can be, they do attack at night like that and bats in the Astral can also have associations with black magic. But animals attacking can also symbolize egos that are attacking.

While creating the circle of protection, do I also have to say the statement three times or is only the circle to be created three times?

You have to say the statement three times and draw the circle three times as well.

I understand that negative entities not only affect us in the Astral, but the physical plane too. Can we use a conjuration and the circle of protection in the physical plane also to keep negative entities away?

Yes, you can also use the conjurations and circle of protection in the physical plane to keep negative entities away if you feel you need to.

Will the circle of protection keep negative entities away from only me, or will it protect all the persons I work with?

The circle can protect everyone inside it as long as no one goes in or out of it and breaks it.

Can I create a circle of protection for others even if I am not in the circle? If I can, what will be the statement?

Yes, you can draw it around others even if you are not in it. You say everything the same as when you draw it around yourself except that instead of asking it to be drawn around yourself, you ask for it to be drawn around the people.

Since my Lord is Christ (not the lesser god, Jupiter), how am I going to protect myself when I Astral travel?

I cannot, therefore, invoke Jupiter for protection because I don't believe in lesser gods. Can I invoke Christ for protection instead?

Jupiter is another name for the 'Father' and he is very important in Christianity. These are just names for the same thing; it's not worth getting stuck over them. If you stick to the rigid confines of a religion you will not be able to progress esoterically. If you want to be an esotericist you have to ask yourself what you really know and whether you only want to believe, because experience is needed to discover the truth. If you try this conjuration you will see that it works.

As I lay in bed, right before the Astral split, in the moment of paralysis, a form descended on me in my bed. I fought out of fear at first and tried to fight it off, but I felt nothing there. Then finally I felt an arm wrap around me and I touched it (in my Astral body). It was not threatening, but benign and unthreatening.

Last night I laid upon the couch and drifted off. At the moment of the split, and the paralysis, I felt an animal that seemed like a cat, jump upon the couch and lay upon me. I tried out of fear to smack it away but nothing was there, only making myself move to regain bodily control. This repeated over and over until I let the fear go and then I could feel it. I was feeling it with my Astral arms, not the physical ones.

The first step is in learning how our Astral bodies are different from our physical, and that we don't move them the same way. I am learning, albeit in small steps, but the most amazing thing about it is that someone is helping me, showing me things. I am slowly but surely going down a new road and I am growing into much more than I was before.

There are negative entities that use that very common Astral experience known as sleep paralysis to frighten people and put them off the Astral and esoteric things. They sometimes take the shape of animals; it could be that this is what you are seeing. To check this, use the conjuration all the way through and see what happens to the entity.

Since this lecture, every night before I hit the pillow, I have conjured the house and asked for a circle of protection around the entire house. Although I have not knowingly experienced anything that would indicate I needed to protect my house in this manner before now, I try to be

diligent and practice what I'm learning.

After forgetting to conjure away and draw the circle one night, everything you said came true and I have no hesitation in heeding every word of advice offered on this subject!

As I said, I have never knowingly been troubled by negative entities before, but it seems that now they know what I'm up to, they really are out to annoy me!

Yes, they really are there. There is a huge war going on between the forces of light and darkness. Most of this is unknown to the average person.

Having the right tools is enabling me to observe aspects of fear and have the potential to deal effectively with each issue that arises. I agree that ultimately there isn't actually anything to fear - it's just a matter of proving it to myself, which gives me solid confidence.

In your experience, is an individual's level of spiritual development likely to be tested to the same degree by negative entities?

The more we progress spiritually, the more the negative entities attack us and try to stop us. They see us then as people who are getting away from their grip and who begin to pose a threat to them.

The further into the light we go, the more the darkness comes against us.

I am glad to get these tools. I have had several friends who have become very involved in the psychic without really having any interest in the spiritual work that must go along with it. Without an exception, they have all been negatively influenced by it within a couple of years. I was interested in such things at first myself, but was always

more interested in self-awareness and knowledge than in the psychic and other 'parlor games'. I had a situation a couple of years ago with a friend who had developed her clairvoyant skills fairly highly, and had put together an informal class dealing with different topics. I didn't take it too seriously and out of curiosity decided to attend.

I had been working with awareness and self-knowledge, but didn't take seriously the need to protect myself. One night I attended her class, but in the early hours of the morning I was awakened with a strange sensation. It's very difficult to explain the sensation, but similar to an extreme shame or ego attack.

Now, I'm not prone to huge bouts of shame or anxiety, but not knowing what was going on I didn't halt it soon enough. After a while, I realized it was an attack, and I was able to stop it immediately, but, not soon enough and by the time I woke up, I was physically sick. I literally felt de-energized for months.

It taught me a very valuable lesson/s though. Don't set yourself up for these attacks. Protect yourself. Practice awareness. Don't be where (if you can help it) these influences are being called upon. I wouldn't go around classes such as that, for anything.

You are quite right about those entities and about dealing with them and avoiding harmful places.

Self-knowledge is a vital basis for development, because the esoteric Path is all about inner transformation, but it is important to protect yourself psychically.

I was just wondering whether these are things that must be said aloud, or may be said silently in the mind.

You say them aloud, because the word has strength and because then you do it aloud in a dream or in the Astral too and it has more power there.

It depends on the situation in the physical though, because there are many times when you have to pronounce it silently.

At one stage I remember rising slowly towards the ceiling from my bed. Then all of a sudden I heard a very evil growl right beside me. It was what I thought at the time to be my cat, but my cat is only a kitten and I remember thinking "This can't be my kitten making such a noise." Anyway, I remember this growl was stopping me from fully projecting and then it was simply over. Does this sound like a negative entity? I didn't really feel scared at the time because I thought to myself that this isn't real and I said for it to go away. But then I felt it was quite over-powering and I didn't succeed to project.

Yes, it was a negative entity. If you had used Bellilin then it would have gone away. As it was it succeeded in its attempt to stop you in the Astral. Next time you will have learned from this one and will be able to get rid of anything negative that appears.

When the two (angelic) people turned up to the course and showed special powers, were these powers seen in the physical?

These powers were mostly seen in the Astral at the time, but there were reports in the newspaper by people who had seen the woman hovering in the air in the physical. The dark side always likes to show off powers.

How did they obtain these powers? Were they tricked by other negative entities? Was there a transfer of energy?

They consciously awakened in evil, just as some of us here are working to awaken in light.

Do these powers manifest in all of us already (positive and negative)?

Not usually. These powers have to be developed, although the forces of light and darkness exist within everyone.

What would have happened to them if they had resorted to doing good rather than evil?

They would have had to repent and want to change. Then they would have had to start the esoteric work from the beginning like everyone else.

Would they have still disappeared in the physical after doing good and re-joined the Wheel of Samsara, or remained in the Astral off the Wheel?

They would start in the physical like anyone else and stay on the Wheel unless they eventually managed to progress far enough to get off.

Is using the circle of protection and conjurations around newborn babies beneficial in saving them from the harm of negative entities and their egos from previous lives?

Yes, it can be beneficial to protect them from outside evil entities, although they are much less susceptible to attack than adults because fewer of their egos have manifested and their essence (consciousness) manifests more.

Is there any shield of protection that moves with you, without breaking, to protect you from sinister beings?

There is a work with an elemental of a Century plant (Agave Americanas), which gives a more all-round protection; this is given in a later course.

Last night I resumed working on trying to Astral travel in accordance with this week's assigned practices and I have had some success! I began by doing the conjuration and casting the magical circle and then I recited the mantra Fa Ra On, which I haven't tried before.

I must have gone straight to sleep, but after about an hour I found that I was awake in the middle of a dream and began walking around and doing things as though awake! While walking around I found that I was able to walk through things. It was then that a bad entity attacked me. I was grabbed from behind. I turned around and saw that it was non-human - possibly an ego as I think I have seen it before. So I applied the Jupiter conjuration and it worked! After saying it three times the entity disappeared. Then I did some flying.

I still haven't been able to Astral travel straight away by rising out of the body, but continue to work on it. However, I have succeeded in remembering and using the conjurations so I am feeling pleased.

That's good. Keep working towards Astral projection like this and it's likely to be just a matter of time before you get it.

I have had experiences where I was threatened by beings. In these experiences I seem to be conscious that I am dreaming/in the Astral when I am threatened. I still feel unclear as to when it is an experience in the Astral, or whether it is my subconscious producing these experiences. Is there a way to tell?

You get to know whether something is real or whether it is a projection from the subconscious with progress in the elimination of the egos (the elements of the subconscious) and Alchemy. If you do these things then experience and your intuition will also assist you.

In any case, you should use the conjurations if you see any negative entities and are aware enough to; then you will get rid of them.

I had a strange experience last night, while asleep. I woke up suddenly after a vision of a rock band in black. I recognized one of the people in it from the past. I woke up feeling I was being shown negative beings. It felt like it was connected to my questioning at the moment regarding negative entities.

I still find it difficult to differentiate whether it has come from my own subconscious or from the Astral. Should I be going with the initial feelings when I wake up? I have found several times in this course that I have my questions answered in dreams. Is this a reliable source? Is it common?

Go with the initial feeling you had when you woke up. Information is given through dreams so you need to be able to differentiate between those and projections from the subconscious.

Answers to problems are quite common in dreams; that is the place where we get direct teachings. Things do get clearer though with the elimination of the egos and the whole esoteric work in general.

While trying a practice of Astral projection, I saw dark shapes (shadowy, dark clouds) moving around the room. In fear I snapped out of the practice feeling very scared.

Fear is something that can be overcome. The negative things you perceived could have come from your subconscious, although they are more likely to be negative entities in the Astral. To deal with them in future use the conjurations.

Can you really be sure of the nature of Bodhisattvas? I would like to share my story. My brother's son had what was said to be an imaginary friend. I discovered in that month that it was not imaginary.

As I slept one evening, I was awakened to the sensation of a child-sized figure jumping up and down on me. When I began to awaken, it ran away giggling - yet there was no one physically there in my room with me.

A couple of nights later, my father experienced the same encounter, and testified to it without first hearing of my own encounter. My father was a total skeptic of all things paranormal. This spirit paid visits to me for over a year, and after a time, the sleep disruptions became irritating and I was no longer a willing participant in the games.

The spirit came to me again, this time appearing in a strange, cherubic form. It said, "I don't want to be dead anymore. You need to open up so I can get in." I began to realize that this spirit was no innocent little boy. It was evil, if not a fully-fledged demon.

My point is that these Bodhisattvas may not be what they appear.

You are confusing a negative entity with a Bodhisattva; what you saw was a negative entity. As you have experienced, there are many negative entities wishing to deceive anyone who is searching for knowledge. That's why it's important to learn to use the conjurations to check whether something is good or bad and to know what the esoteric Path is.

A true Bodhisattva is a person in the physical world who has built all their solar bodies and has incarnated their Master or Spirit. If someone has this (they are extremely rare), you can invoke their Master or Being who is part of them and who looks like them and he will appear. 'Master' is a title that a person

(Bodhisattva) earns, when incarnating their Master or Spirit. But the Master is a name to describe the Being or a spiritual Being generally, so you should try not to confuse the person who has just been given the title of 'Master' on the Path with a fully awakened spiritual Being residing in the higher dimensions. The person becomes a vehicle for their own Master to manifest within them and receive the title 'Master', but they, while still on the Path, are not the Master itself - that is the Being from the higher dimension.

If in doubt when you call a Master (a spiritual Being from the higher dimensions), you should use the conjurations to check whether the Being is good or evil. If it was evil, it would have gone or become disabled, so you invoke the Master again until the spiritual one appears.

The Master has its own name, the immortal name, which is not usually the physical name of the Bodhisattva (Jeshua Ben Pandira - Jesus, is one of the exceptions to this, as his Master's name was given to his physical mother before his physical birth).

You can only call people (Bodhisattvas) by the name of their Master when they have their Master incarnated. Then they can turn up with the Master within, or at other times just the Master without the Bodhisattva will appear.

By the end of the Path however, the Bodhisattva and the Master become fully integrated.

Week Seven Exercises

The Conjurations and the Circle of Protection

This Week's Exercise

Practice and use the Conjurations and the Circle of Protection

Learn the conjurations by listening carefully to the sound files and repeating them time and time again until you have learnt them by heart. It is important that you have the conjurations memorized at the tip of your tongue. This way you will be far more likely to use them in the Astral plane. It won't help at all if you're in the Astral plane before an entity and you cannot remember all the words - it just won't work. Therefore, take care in learning the conjurations and the circle of protection well, so that you can make good use of them in the Astral plane. Pay particular attention to the singing tone of the conjuration of Bellilin.

Useful Tips when using the Conjurations and the Circle of Protection

1. If an entity tries to frighten you as you are coming out of your body, right in the moment of projection or during the sleep paralysis, you should not move or try to end the exercise out of fear. You need to behave as though you have not heard or seen anything and without worrying or moving. Sing the conjuration of Bellilin to get rid of the entity.

2. If you are not sure whether you have drawn the circle of protection well, start again. If you need to start the conjurations from the beginning, you should do that too.

3. If you are conjuring an entity and the entity begins to mock your conjuration, the entity is trying to undermine your confidence. You need to be focused when you are saying it.

Extra Astral Projection Exercises

Following on from last week's mantra exercises there are two more mantras to try this week. They are the mantra Fa Ra On and the mantra Tai Re Re Re Re.

The Mantra Fa Ra On

Don't forget about the option to visualize the Pyramids of Egypt when you try this exercise. The visualization exercises you have been using on the course so far could by now be helping your ability to visualize. Some students like this mantra because it keeps their mind focused on the Pyramids.

The Mantra Tai Re Re Re Re

For this mantra, you really need to listen carefully to the sound files because this mantra has a singing tone. There are students who have had very good results with this mantra.

Summary of This Week's Exercises

1. The Conjurations and the Circle of Protection
Practice them as explained in the topic enough times so that they are recorded in your subconscious and you can do them in the Astral.

2. Astral Projection Exercises
The mantras to use this week are Fa Ra On for the first three days of the week and then Tai Re Re Re Re for the next three days of the week.

3. Vocalizing Mantras
Pronounce the mantra Fa Ra On and Tai Re Re Re Re for 20 minutes or more at a different time from your Astral projection exercise.

4. Waking Up in Dreams Exercise
Questioning where you are, ask whether you are in the physical world or in the Astral world by using the jump and pulling your finger.

5. Remember Your Dreams
Use the mantra Raom Gaom or remain still when you wake up and go back over the night's dreams.

6. Visualizing an Object for 10 Minutes Each Day
This is an optional exercise. Pick an object of your choice for your visualization exercise for this week and do it for at least 10 minutes each day.

Week 8

ASTRAL AND DREAM EXPERIENCES

*I*n this topic we are going to look into what happens in dreams and in the Astral, how you can understand the things you see and experience there, and the kind of things that you can best do while you are consciously in the Astral plane.

The language of the Astral is intuitive and symbolic, so to understand it you need to develop and use your intuition, gain experience of being there and progress along the esoteric Path thereby awakening psychic faculties and consciousness.

There are two guides to supplement this topic: one on the meaning of symbols and another on the meaning of numbers.

You can also get a basic understanding to start with by reading the information given on the Journey to Enlightenment course. So by the time you complete that you should have a wider understanding of the esoteric work, because basically in the Astral everything relates to that.

Using Intuition

It is most important to use intuition when interpreting the meaning of a dream or an Astral experience because of the intuitive and symbolic nature of the language of the Astral. Each symbol there can have many different meanings. Each is relevant to the one who experiences them even though there are symbols with universal meanings.

Intuition is a sense that allows us to capture information from a higher plane that could not otherwise be gained from the mind or from the five senses. The information reaches us from a spiritual part within that is located in the higher dimensions. It is one of several psychic faculties that can be developed on these courses and can be very useful to have.

Intuition works immediately. When you remember a dream you get a first feeling about what things mean. Go with that feeling without allowing the mind to come in and reason, because the ordinary mind lacks that higher connection.

We can be forewarned of danger and other things because events that are going to happen often take place in the higher dimensions first, and information from those dimensions can reach us here.

Everyone carries this sense to a certain extent and probably most have experienced it. The problem however, is that most people do not develop it or pay attention to it. The Searching Within course explains how to activate it, while the Journey to Enlightenment course explains how to develop and awaken it and other faculties, but everyone has it, so begin to use it when you want to discover the meaning of a dream or Astral experience.

Symbols in the Astral Plane and in Dreams

Much of what is seen in dreams in the beginning of the work are the projections of the subconscious, so intuition should be used to tell where they are coming from. It is very important to learn about the subconscious and how the psyche works because then you can take the steps to clear the elements of the subconscious, which we call 'egos'.

Without this, Astral experiences are always subject to the subjective projections of the subconscious.

Generally dreams and Astral experiences have a symbolic side. If you look at a dream plainly there may be nothing much to it, but when you recall your first intuitive feeling about it when you wake up, you know that it is referring to a certain aspect of your life - it is giving information about a person, a situation, etc and you know what it is and what is going to happen. In this way, you gradually begin to interpret your dreams and experiences and the symbols in them. It is very useful for inner development, because as you gradually remember your dreams more and more, you intuitively know that a particular dream is telling you what aspect in your life you must change, what egos you urgently need to work upon, which situations are harming you, or are harming others, etc.

In the Astral, a particular symbol may sometimes have different meanings and the right one can be grasped through intuition. It's important though, not to tell any esoteric symbols that you may see in the Astral to anyone, because secrecy is very important there and if you tell others, whoever they are, you may not be shown any more for some time. It's known as hermetic silence.

What to Do in the Astral

It is very easy to waste an opportunity to learn something important when you go to the Astral. Time spent flying around nowhere in particular, looking at details on walls, etc, is not the best way to use an Astral experience. It is better to get esoteric experiences.

Sometimes these experiences are given anyway and are there when you Astral travel. For example, you may wake up in the Astral in a situation that is full of symbolic meanings for you. At other times, however, you have to seek out the learning.

This can be done by following your intuition or by asking your divine Being (either the male or female aspects of the Being known as the Divine Mother or Father) to take you where you need to go. Then either of them can take you somewhere.

Or you can go to a temple to be taught. If you know one concentrate upon it or ask your divine Being to take you to the Gnostic temple to be taught. Don't be surprised if you are not allowed in, because often a certain level of esoteric work is needed to get into many of them.

Another option is to invoke a Master. These are spiritual beings who are awake in the higher dimensions. By invoke I mean to call or summon, and that is to call an external Being, not for anything to arrive and to come into you - that is channeling and that allows external entities to come into your body and is not recommended.

You may know of some Masters already and can invoke them, but be warned, because some that you have read about could now have fallen and be a demon, since they can rise and fall. At other times a negative entity can appear first, even in the appearance of a Master, so you need to use the conjurations if you are in any doubt.

Everyone has their own Master, but that is not present

within your average person and does not show itself until the appropriate time after it has been incarnated, which is when someone progresses enough along the esoteric Path. Then the person gets the title 'Master' but it is the part of the Being that is really a Master. But for people who have not incarnated it, the only option is to call another Master.

Bear in mind that people can call themselves Masters here in the physical world but they have not incarnated their Being and therefore do not have the true esoteric title of 'Master'. So calling them in the Astral is a waste of time and can easily lead to being deceived. If a person has incarnated their Master, the Master has the appearance of the person in the physical world.

Traveling

There are different ways to travel somewhere in the Astral and using your intuition at the time is a good guide. You can always walk in the Astral, but it's much quicker to fly. You can be taken somewhere if you ask, or you can concentrate upon a specific place and go there immediately, or travel from the spot you are in using what you see there to guide you. If you want to go back to a place you have been to before, visualize it and you can go there.

It is possible to concentrate upon a place and project directly there, or as you go to sleep, you may see dream images. If you concentrate upon one of them, going into it with your visualization, you can go directly into it and be there consciously in the Astral, or you can go back there in a dream and continue your learning.

If you are already in a place in which you are being taught, it's usually better to stay there and continue the learning unless it is time to go.

Don't worry about getting stuck in the Astral. We always come back unless the physical body dies: you just wake up from sleep, or more often, straight away after the experience. The difficulty is staying in the Astral without going back to the body. It helps to hold onto something there, to stay aware, which will help prevent the conscious experience becoming a dream, and to watch the emotions, since any emotion can bring you back quickly. Emotions such as fear and worry are major culprits.

If you get there and can't see, conjure away; an ego or a negative entity could be the problem.

Sometimes in the Astral a Being can appear in front of you, sometimes telling you different things. Through intuition you can tell if that Being is good or evil just by looking at them and using that sense. If you look into their eyes, you can often tell what they are, because their eyes can uncover the evil ones. If you have negativity towards someone however, your subconscious can make you see them as a negative entity anyway, or negative entities can use your dislike of the person to portray them as a negative entity in order to fool you. So work on the subconscious (egos) is vital.

Through the process of the esoteric Path, the consciousness is gradually awakened. That means that you clear the consciousness of those elements (egos) that make up the subconscious. Then you are more aware in daily life and more aware in dreams until the consciousness is awakened.

The level of teachings that someone gets is entirely due to their capacity to understand and receive them. This is according to the level of spiritual development that one has, which you can learn to make progress with on the Journey to Enlightenment course.

The real way to get profound wisdom and understanding is to take up the esoteric Path. The capacity for wisdom contained in the ordinary consciousness is very limited. The knowledge about oneself and life that is attainable is small for an ordinary person compared with what it is possible to achieve on the Path.

On the Path, spiritual beings in their influence through the higher dimensions upon the three-dimensional world and hence upon events of everyday life, place events and situations so that the person can be tested - situations that test how the person acts in relation to anger or honesty, for instance. By doing this, the spiritual beings can see how prepared someone is to receive true knowledge. It is not given just to anyone because then it is not valued and is easily rubbished and abused.

Knowledge is given according to one's own merits, when someone is prepared for it, and has earned it. It's given according to the capacity and level of spiritual development of the person. Nasty, angry, and dishonest people for example, are restricted in their capacity to receive true knowledge. If they reduce these defects properly, their capacity to receive knowledge can then have a chance to be increased.

Questions & Answers

Q. On a recent Astral experience, I was taken somewhere and I was shown some things I did not understand at the time. The first was of what appeared to be an ancient wall. On this wall were round objects that upon closer observation became scenes of different people and different times. The only thing that comes to mind is the Wheel of Samsara. Was this an esoteric symbol to teach me?

A. Yes, this very much sounds like symbols that were used in the Astral to teach you. If you don't understand them now, remember them very well, so that later if you continue this work and your capacity - your consciousness increases, along with the information that you get from these courses, you will find that you can understand the things which seemed to be obscure in the beginning.

Does the infinity symbol have any significance? Likewise, does classical music have any significance?

The infinity symbol has a meaning; it is a true esoteric symbol. It represents the cycles of evolution and devolution, which travel round and round, represented by the figure eight, from existence to existence. The real spiritual work is needed to get off this cycle.

The symbol can be found in the Ninth Sphere, which means that the work with Alchemy needs to be carried out. Classical music can be spiritual; there is music in the higher dimensions, which is very significant to certain experiences. The symbol of infinity is an esoteric symbol, so you shouldn't say anything about these kinds of things to anyone if you see them in the Astral. They are given to the individual and if they are spoken about, darkness follows and you may not be shown things. In the esoteric world the ability to be silent is important.

When you say not to mention anything about these symbols, does that include to you in these questions and answers or just in my everyday life?

I've had no real new experience since this one. Is this because I spoke about it (also I've been quite sick and run down with a bad tooth ache so hopefully this is the reason)? Because of the above, I didn't do my exercises for about a week, I see what you mean about losing what you built up very quickly.

It includes everyone, but distinguish between ordinary experiences and the proper esoteric ones.

Both speaking about personal esoteric information and illness can bring about the loss of valuable experiences. When the continuity in the exercises is lost, it needs to be built up again. Don't force the body to practice when you are ill though.

A comment of yours in your lecture on dreams struck me as being strange at the time. You said that it may be useful to keep a diary of your dreams but to keep it secret. If I see symbols in the future and keep a record of them, is this okay as long as I keep it secret?

Yes, you shouldn't have any problems with writing things in the diary as long as you keep them secret. Putting them in a code known only to yourself, for example, can help.

The other night was the first time I have ever consciously got up in the Astral. I made the conscious decision to gently roll out of bed. I wasn't even sure it worked, but then it was as if the lights came on and I was somewhere else. I took that little jump and floated along effortlessly through walls and any object. I went through a plate glass window and hovered above the trees. I did not know where to go since I did not know where I was.

This confusion brought me back to the comfort of my bed. I went back in the Astral several more times as I often do, but when I tried to pass through a different wall, I thudded to the floor. Is this common? What was holding me back the next few times? It was as if the walls were solid!

The problem with the wall was your mind; doubts cause that problem. Push into the wall with your hand so that it starts to go through; then follow through with the rest of your body.

I've heard that you should be careful when shape shifting in the Astral because you could come back with a part of that animal and start developing some of its wild characteristics. I would really appreciate your comments on this. Is there danger there?

No, you can't come back as an animal by doing that; what you are doing has nothing to do with the process of birth and death. You would do best to forget about shape shifting because it is a projection of the mind. Go into the Astral clear of that and get some real spiritual teachings.

First Supplementary Topic: General Dream Symbol Guide

*H*ere is a guide to the meaning of some symbols that are given in the Astral and dreams. The starting point for some of it was found in the work of Samael Aun Weor, who gave many symbols in his books. I have included the things that I have been able to verify myself. You can use it as a general guide only, because there are other meanings to many of the symbols. Much depends upon the particular circumstances of the experiences too and using your own intuition is vital.

Also bear in mind that objects that you see may or may not have a symbolic meaning; many things may be representations of the mind, and may have no value. Again, your intuition will guide you if you have practiced enough and can use it.

There are no discussions on the courses related to symbols, because they are for the dreamer to discover their meaning. Also because I don't want to spend my time as a dream guide. It is better for me to explain about the esoteric world in general, to show how to walk along the Path, to give the tools to do so and to teach you how to learn to understand the meaning of your own dreams and Astral experiences rather than you having to rely each time upon what someone else says. Esoteric knowledge is something personal to each individual and something that an individual acquires with their own efforts.

I have not included many things of the Path (the Three Mountains) because they have their own process, but there are general things that a beginner or someone just starting the work is likely to encounter, although most things are still relevant to those who are on the Path. Some of the things in the guide you will not have information about on this course; they will be made clearer by doing the Journey to Enlightenment course.

Where there is a description that says something simple or general, for example "how one appears internally", you need to look at what is present in the dream and its context to get your own information on it.

Many incidents in dreams are the actions of egos or the representations/images of the mind and these need to be distinguished from situations where genuine symbols are given.

The Guide

A

Age: If divine beings talk about age in their places of learning in the higher dimensions, they are talking about Initiations.

Agony: To see yourself in agony - material progress, your social and financial situation will improve.

Amusement Park: The illusory life of the egos.

Angel: The presence of a Master.

Anger: The manifestation of this ego. You cannot pass the test of fire (on the preparatory Path before the Path of Initiation) with this.

Airplane: It represents how one's spiritual progress is going.

Ark: Alchemy.

Army: There are armies of the White Lodge and of the Black Lodge. The egos also form the legion. A fight against an evil army represents the legion of egos, armies of darkness, enemies. If you form part of a good army look at your grade in it, it represents the level of work of the dreamer.

Authorities of the Law: If they are against the dreamer it is divine justice in action, Karma. If in favor of the dreamer then the divine law protects him/her.

B

Balloons: An ordinary life, not on the Path, mundane.

Banquet: A celebration of a spiritual progress.

Barriers: Obstacles and difficulties.

Bathing: In pure clean water - Alchemical cleaning. In dirty water - illness.

Beard: For a man it indicates power. Any anomaly in the beard is a bad sign. In a woman it indicates sexual degeneration.

Bicycle: How you are traveling spiritually.

Birds: In a cage means that there are elements that have come to fulfill a mission, but they are locked by the ego; with the death of the egos they are set free.

Blow (as in punching): To receive blows without a reason - attacks.

Body: This can show the state of the physical or internal bodies.

Bread: Christic atoms.

Broom: To clean yourself. Modification of habits and customs. Elimination of Egos. An old broom – one step to eliminating a defect.

A Building: Represents where you are or where you need to reach with your spiritual work (transmutation). It is where you inhabit spiritually. A white one means purification, death of the egos.

Bull: The masculine principle, but usually the ego.

Bullets: If someone is shooting them at you - insults directed towards you. If you are shooting them carelessly or wrongly - bad thoughts; there is a need to control the Mental body.

C

Canal: The spinal column. A dry canal represents the absence of Kundalini in the spine.

Cane: The same as canal above.

Car: Symbolizes the inner work one is doing in the physical and shows how it is going. A couple can ride in the car when people are married - then it is related to them. Look at the type of car, its color and condition, how you drive it, etc.

Castle: Fortress. Negative castle - a stronghold of evil.

Cat: If it attacks - enemies. Black cat - black magic. On the positive side a cat can also be related to the sexual fire.

Catastrophe: It is related to the number 16. It is very bad and represents a fall or a descent spiritually.

Cave: A cavern of the mind, with all its darkness.

Century Plant (Agave Americanas, Fique plant): You are being attacked by the forces of darkness and need to protect yourself.

Chains: To break chains – to free yourself.

Chalice: The brain, the female sexual organs.

Chicken: A frightened chicken - egos of fear and weakness.

Child: A spiritual part within.

Church: A spiritual place - look at the context.

Classroom: Being taught in the internal worlds by Masters. Also look at your behavior in the classroom.

Cliff: Falling down a cliff symbolizes an esoteric fall backwards, but it is also used in the test of air in the probative Path (the Path before the Path of Initiations).

Clock: Time is pressing – look at the time in terms of the sum of the numbers as stated in the topic on the meaning of numbers.

Clothes: Indicates one's spiritual state or grade. Dressed in rags - spiritually bad, misery and pain. Internal bodies.

Coins: Payments for deeds, Dharmic credits. Refer the number to the Kabalistic sum of the coins.

Cold (as in temperature): Solitude, sadness. Bitterness.

Column: Support of the internal temple.

Combat: Fights against the egos and enemies. If it is a fight against enemies, it is a bad sign to loose. Fighting with yourself - fight against the egos.

Comet: Heralds impending disaster; you have to be careful.

Cow: The feminine principle. A white cow represents the Divine Mother, a black cow represents her opposite.

Cross: Work with the Alchemy, sacrifices.

Crow: Negative forces threaten internally: you must protect yourself appropriately. Black magic.

D

Dagger: The internal assassination of the Christ, fornication. Not to be confused with a sword, which represents the Kundalini rising, nor with a short sword with a white handle, which is given when the Kundalini begins to rise.

Darkness: To be in the darkness indicates lack of consciousness in the internal worlds although it can also be due to the egos or negative entities. In the latter case it can be cleared with the conjurations.

Dates: They should be worked out through the Kabalistic numbers. They announce important things.

Dawn: A beginning, inspiration, a new start.

Death: If you see yourself dead, it means the death of a defect (ego) or defects. To unearth yourself - a new ego is born. In some situations seeing someone else dead or finding out about it could also refer to the death of the ego or to their physical death.

Debts: Karma is being applied to you. Karmic payments have to be made.

Defecation: Decrease of psychological defects (egos).

Dirty: A bad sign for the future. Inner filth. The danger of death for a sick person.

Disabled: To see yourself disabled or crippled - the essence is crippled. Lame - a lack of sacrifice for humanity.

Desert: Aridness and solitude on the Path.

Devil: Lucifer the psychological trainer, the tempter.

Doctor: Help from the Masters of medicine in the case of illness.

Dog: There are two types of dog: the negative one steals the sexual energies, the other is a guide along the Alchemical work. Dogs can also be guards.

Donkey: The inferior Mental body; the ordinary mind. To ride upon it shows control of the mind.

Dove: A white dove is the Holy Spirit.

E

Eagle: The Father.

Elephant: It means the humility that one must have. The taller the elephant the more humble one needs to be.

Exams: Spiritual/esoteric tests. Watch how you study and prepare for them, how you sit them and the results achieved.

F

Face (your own): How you appear internally.

Father: Representation of the eternal Father who teaches.

Flying: A certain type and level of consciousness achieved.

What is seen and felt while flying needs to be interpreted. In general it's a good sign; it's even better when someone wakes up fully into the Astral from a dream, although it can be given as a help when someone is doing badly in order to give them a boost.

Fire: Gives light or destroys, so it depends how it is seen.

Fish (cooked): Served in the plate - abundance of food. Decomposed - illnesses.

Fisherman: Walker of the Path, who spreads the teaching.

Flag: It represents success. Pay attention to the state of it.

G

Garden (pleasant): Spiritual happiness.

H

Hair (of the head): The state of one's sexual energies and spiritual state. A bald head - lost energies.

Hat: New - joy. To put one on - quick trip. If it is not white - spiritually bad. A friend who goes away. Loss of power.

Harvesting: The fruit of one's own deeds. If bad - there is a need to learn to sow.

Hell: To be in one of the circles of the infra-dimensions. Indicates one's inner level, depending on the situation. To be unconscious there shows that the dreamer needs to work hard to eliminate the negative heavy states that drag him or her there. It is possible to investigate there consciously, to go there to learn too. Being put into Hell is a sign of a present or future reality. To get out of there shows some success and hope.

Horse: It represents the work in the physical as a car does. To be mounted on a horse indicates spiritual advancement. If the horse is well decorated, it indicates a good sign. A runway horse is spiritually dangerous.

House: The work that one builds. If built on sand for example, the work has dodgy foundations and can easily fall. If it is inhabited by strangers it shows egos.

I

Insects: Larvae in the Astral body. There is a need to carry out a cleaning internally; clean the Astral body with the awakened fire. They also represent attacks.

J

Jackal: Anubis judging, Karma to pay.

Jewels: Depressing news. When taken out of a chest, a good sign.

Judge/Judgment: Being judged by the Masters of Karma in the internal worlds. If the judgment is in our favor, a Karmic matter goes our way. If the judgment goes against us, there is Karma to pay.

K

Killing: Usually refers to the elimination of the egos, but watch who is killed: it is possible to go against the spiritual.

L

Lake: Related to sexual transmutation.

Lamb: The son, the Christ.

Lion: Represents the law of Karma. The Solar man in its ascended aspect. A vicious lion represents the violent egos. Killing a fierce lion with your bare hands is triumph over certain sexual passions.

Light: Excellent omen. Immediate help; material and spiritual improvement.

Loan: Good if it is approved and sensible, but remember that it needs to be paid. Business with the Karmic law (divine law).

Lustful Dreams: Due to a lack of work on the egos of lust - urgent need to overcome them. Indifference in front of lust shows some chastity and balanced psychic centers.

Lustful Odor: Lustful people emit a bad odor in the Astral.

M

Marriage: Physical death, either of the person who dreams they are getting married or of the person they dream is getting married. However, when the person is married physically (often as a newlywed) and dreams of being in a married relationship with their physical partner it means achievements in the Alchemical transmutation: they form a true couple. Marriage can also be part of Initiation ceremonies for those at the appropriate place on the Initiatic Path.

Master: A spiritual Being - will teach though not always in the way you may think. For example, if a Master is in silence you have asked a silly question.

Mother: Represents the internal Divine Mother.

Mirror: How you appear in a mirror represents how you appear internally.

Money: This depends on the context, it could for example be related to greed if you are stealing it, or it could be cosmic money related to the Karmic payments.

Monsters: Demons, egos. The dreamer is in the infra-dimensions, in Hell. Also, a monster is faced in the first test of the Initiatic Path - the Guardian of the Threshold.

Moon: Represents the negative part of yourself.

Mountain: Initiation, difficulties, hard task. It is a good sign to climb one. It also means the goal.

Mud: A bad sign, a lack of death of the egos, negative influences. To get muddy - illnesses, need to eliminate egos.

N

Nails: In good condition - a comfortable life. Ugly and dirty - miseries. Broken - illnesses. Long – triumph.

Naked: Big troubles and/or difficulties are going to fall upon you. Look at what you go through too when naked.

Nightmares: Indicate a bad psychological state or an upset stomach. The dreamer is in the infra-dimensions.

Numbers: They are interpreted Kabalistically.

O

Owl: Can represent both wisdom and negative forces.

P

Pact: Pay careful attention if you have signed a document or made a verbal pact with anyone, because if it is done without consciousness it could have been made with the forces of darkness.

Parents: Representation of the Divine Father and Mother. To dream of parents is not necessarily a good sign; they often only appear as a last resort when the student is doing very badly. It's important to pay careful attention to what they say and do.

Path: A pathway in general means the esoteric Path, Initiation. If it is steep and difficult it is the direct Path of Initiation. But not all are the true Path. If it is a dark one, be careful. If it is in a spiral and ascending it is the Path to Nirvana, without sacrifices.

Peacock: Arrogance.

Pig: Filth, laziness, fornication. There is a need to work upon yourself.

Pine: The Father.

Police: The divine law actively working. To be arrested - Karma to pay. This is sorted out in the Tribunal of Divine Justice. Arresting someone - Karma acts upon that person. You pay or they pay you for your sacrifices.

Poster: Read the information on it.

Prison Cell: The law of Karma acts. Psychological prison. The egos have one locked without freedom.

Punishment: Paying a Karmic debt.

R

Ram: Success or failure of the dreamer. Still - favorable. Fat - abundance. Thin - scarcity. To fall from a ram that is walking with the dreamer is to harm a friend.

Rain: Tears, sadness and negative emotions. To walk under the rain - bitterness, pain, suffering.

Recurring Dream: Something needs to be worked out.

Red Beret or Turban: An Initiate of the Black Lodge.

Rock: Alchemical foundation of the work.

S

Scales: The divine law and justice.

School: The school of life. Look at the context to see how you are doing in it in relation to your esoteric work.

Sea: The sexual waters. Calm and clean - good control of the waters, chastity. Turbulent and dark - passion or lust.

Seed: An invitation or potential to be born spiritually.

Sentry: If watchful - alert consciousness. If the sentry is asleep - unconsciousness.

Sharks: Egos.

Shoes: How one walks along the Path. Barefoot - doing badly. Inadequate footwear - doing the work improperly, etc.

Smell: How you smell reflects the state of your sexual energies. Sexual energies emit smells; lust smells bad.

Snake: There are two types: the risen Kundalini and the negative tempting serpent. If the latter bites - a sexual fall.

Snow: Achievements with chastity. A bad omen if the dreamer is covered in it or feels cold.

Spear: A phallic symbol. It represents the work with the seminal waters.

Stairs: To go up - spiritual ascent, a beginning, new internal tasks. Being stopped on one - obstacles. Stopping on one - stagnant work. To go down is bad spiritually. To fall off is very bad: it depends of the height from which one falls.

Staff: The Kundalini, the spinal column.

Stars: Refer to what is happening in the sky.

Stigmata's: Received towards the end of the second mountain, but if seen by someone who is not at that stage they indicate pain received while doing the spiritual work. They are very painful but you need to bear the pain somehow.

Stone: Refer to rock.

Studying: Study in life using the esoteric work. Prepare or preparing for tests. Pay attention to the way you are studying.

Sun: The Christ. Success in Initiation. Rising - something needs to be born within. Setting - something needs to die within. Dim or hazy - being obscured by egos. An eclipse of the sun - the egos eclipse and dominate the consciousness; the light is blocked; one does not allow the Being to manifest.

Swim: How you go in the sexual waters, the waters of life. Also used for the test of water on the probative Path.

Sword: The will (willpower). It also represents the awakened Kundalini, not to be confused with a dagger. The sword lengthens as the Kundalini rises higher.

T

Teeth Falling Out: Loss. Also the loss of a relative.

Temple: A place of teachings. Also refers to the physical body in relation to it as a vessel of the Being. Divine protection in a hard setback that the dreamer will suffer. Building of the internal temple. It can also mean that the dreamer becomes the helper of a powerful man.

Thorns: Pain, voluntary suffering. Christic will.

Tigers: They have positive and negative connotations. Positive - wisdom and intelligence. Negative - strong enemies; treason by someone, or that someone is intending to treason you. If you defeat the tiger, the danger is over.

Torch of Fire: Alight – the sexual fire lit/risen.

Train: The work in the physical with the vehicle/ organization that is spreading the teaching. To get off the train is to leave the teaching.

Treasure: To unbury a treasure means to recover esoteric work from the past that has been dormant.

Tremor: Tests. To see a tremor - epidemic and/or collective accident of which the dreamer will take part.

W

War: The fight against enemies/egos.

Water: Sexual energies, transmutation. To be dragged by water indicates spiritual failure and inner weakness. It can also relate to health: being in dirty water indicates illness.

Washing Yourself: A good sign if it is clean water.

Wave: Related to instability in the transmutation - look at the context.

Weapons: Used to fight evil. Acquired when honors and grades are obtained. The negative side has its own weapons.

Wedding: The death of one of the participants (bride or groom). If someone dreams of themselves getting married they are going to die. It may take a long or short time to manifest, but working seriously with the three key elements of the Initiatic Path can alter it.

Wine: Transmuted sexual energy. Generally a good sign, but not if you get drunk with it. Red wine – fight. White wine – joy. Look at its container and drinking vessel.

Worms: Larvae's, decay, degeneration.

Y

Youth: Seeing yourself younger than you really are - longevity.

SECOND SUPPLEMENTARY TOPIC: THE MEANING OF NUMBERS

*N*umbers are used in the Astral world by divine beings to teach. You can therefore see them not only when you are conscious in the Astral but in dreams too.

So pay attention to them and use this guide to assist you in their interpretation. These numbers occur throughout the history of esotericism. They are the basis for the Tarot cards and occur throughout the work of Samael Aun Weor, the founder of modern Gnosis and this list owes much to his work.

Many people see numbers in their dreams, so this guide will be useful; it is just a summary of the numbers and a short guide rather than a complete description. Each number needs to be interpreted according to the context of the experience and the spiritual work the person is doing. Bear in mind that many of the terms used are esoteric; they apply especially to those who have taken up the spiritual Path and are beyond the scope of this course to explain. I have other courses such as the Journey to Enlightenment one, where I explain the knowledge of the inner worlds and the spiritual Path more fully.

The numbers go from 1 to 22. If a number is over 22, you add up its parts. So for example, if you have 23 you add 2 + 3 giving the number 5.

When numbers within the same type of item have been given you add them up together. So for example, if you get $24.48, it breaks down as 2 + 4 + 4 + 8 = 18.

When separate numbers of completely different types of items have been given, you add them up separately and then get the meaning of each separate number. For example 23 stones and 57 footballs break down as 2 + 3 = 5 and 5 + 7 = 12 so you need to look at the meaning of the numbers 5 and 12.

When you are summing up a series of related numbers such as the day, year and month in a birthday, you treat them separately but you sum up to a maximum of 9 for each sub total; you only go over 9 when you add up for the final total. So for example, 11/12/1995 breaks down as 1 + 1 = 2, 1 + 2 = 3, 1 + 9 + 9 + 5 = 24 and then 2 + 4 = 6. The total then will be 2 + 3 + 6 = 11, because in this case, you don't go over the number 9 in a sub total you break the 24 down as 2 + 4 = 6. Then you add up the sub totals, 2 + 3 + 6 = 11.

You only go as far as 12 when summing up hours of the day. So for example, don't use 21:00 hours but 9:00 hours whether it is the morning or the night.

The Numbers

Number 1: The Magician

It represents the masculine principle, the wisdom of the

Father and the unity.

It also represents something that begins (every beginning is difficult and you have to sow to be able to reap).

It also represents the sword, which is willpower and power (that power is the power to awaken and to dominate the passions of the egos).

The 1 unfolds to become 2. The unity is the root of the duality; the Father unfolds into the Mother.

Number 2: The Priestess

The wife of the Magician, the receptive feminine principle.

This is a favorable number.

"The wind and the waves always favor the one who knows how to navigate" (the waves are Alchemical).

The two columns of the temple.

Number 3: The Empress

The divine Mother.

Spiritual and material success and productivity, overcoming obstacles.

The 1 and 2 unfold to produce 3.

Number 4: The Emperor

Ruling, progress, success and mercy.

It also represents stability; establish a solid base in order to succeed.

The cubic stone which is the basis of the spiritual work must be carved.

Number 5: The Hierarch

The divine law, Karma. This includes the person's Karma.

It is also Mars, which is a rigorous spiritual war.

The five-pointed star, the Solar man must be born. Fight so that the star can point upwards.

Number 6: Indecision

The choice between different Paths.

It is also temptation - the struggle between love and desire. The lover.

In triumph - victory, good luck. In failure - erotic violation.

Number 7: Triumph

The chariot of war.

Wars, struggles, battle, difficulties, penitence, pain and bitterness.

One must learn to use the staff and the sword and will thus achieve great victory (willpower is vital).

Number 8: Justice

It signifies hard tests, suffering and pain.

Within it are to be found Initiatic tests and the work of Job, who had enormous patience and who suffered much.

It is also righteousness, justice, and equilibrium. Seek the good, cost what it may. Fulfill the law with good actions.

Number 9: The Hermit

Initiation, solitude and suffering.

The number 9 also represents the Ninth Sphere, the work

with sex. There is great suffering in the Ninth Sphere so one must learn to understand, to suffer and to be resigned. Those who do not will fail.

Number 10: Retribution

The wheel of fortune, successful dealings, changes.

It is also the Wheel of Samsara, the tragic wheel, which is the law of return.

It promises good and bad fortune, ascents and descents, and circumstances which repeat in a different form.

Number 11: Persuasion

The tame lion, the divine law is in your favor.

Have no fear.

Mars.

The work with the fire, with the force of love.

Persuasion has more power than violence, a soft word pacifies anger. Persuasion is in essence, a subtle, spiritual force.

Number 12: The Disciple

It implies sacrifices and sufferings, tests and pain.

Alchemy is vital to take the pain away.

Number 13: Immortality

Death and resurrection, transformations; it indicates total change.

But death has two aspects: the human physical death and the inner death of the egos.

It can also signify something new.

Number 14: Temperance

It is chastity, transmutation, the waters. One must work hard, chiseling the Stone, without which one cannot achieve sexual transmutation.

Matrimonial association, long life, stability, no change.

Number 15: Passion

It warns of danger. Failure in love.

It is the work with the tempter, which esoterically is called Satan or the Devil, in the process of dissolution of the egos.

The passion is based in the Luciferic fire - the main defect is sexual passion, lust.

Number 16: Fragility

The fallen tower; the terrible fall of the initiate.

It brings punishment.

Avoid this date.

Number 17: Hope

Sex under the control of the Spirit.

Number 18: Twilight

Hidden enemies – they can appear at any moment and can be physical or internal.

Illnesses.

Bad for business.

Number 19: Inspiration

The radiant sun, successes, good luck. It promises total

victory, be it through one's own efforts or with the help of other people.

It also can refer to working with the Philosophical Stone.

Number 20: Resurrection

The resurrection of the dead (from the death of the egos comes life, the resurrection of the soul is only possible through Initiation, human beings are spiritually dead and can only resuscitate by means of Initiation).

Favorable changes, take advantage of them. Put an end to weaknesses.

Number 21: Foolishness or Transmutation

The fool: Failure, committing folly in the spiritual work.

Transmutation: It indicates that you must transmute.

Number 22: The Crown of Life

The return to the light, the incarnation of truth within.

Triumph, everything turns out well, power, strength, good fortune.

Additional Information About Clocks

When a clock is shown, the hour is of great importance. A clock signifies that time is pressing, so you need to see the hour. These hours have their own meaning that is different from the other numbers. These numbers refer only to those shown in a clock, although the hours are related to the numbers. The first hour is related to the number 10 and each number goes in that sequence right to the hour 12, which relates to the number 21.

The hour 13 relates to the number 22.

Below is what Samael Aun Weor has written about them.

1st Hour: The transcendental study of occultism.

2nd Hour: Persuasion has more power than violence.

3rd Hour: Serpents, dogs and fire. Work with the Kundalini.

4th Hour: The beginner will wander at night amongst graves; he will suffer the horrors of the visions; he will surrender to Magic and Goecy (he will be attacked in the Astral by millions of black magicians) All this is to move him away from the Path.

5th Hour: Superior waters from heaven. The disciple learns to be chaste and understands the value of the seminal fluid.

6th Hour: Keep still, immobile. The test of the Guardian of the Threshold; courage is needed to defeat him.

7th Hour: The fire comforts the inanimate beings, and if the priest or purified man steals it and projects, if he mixes it in holy oil and consecrates it, he will manage to cure the illnesses by applying it to the affected parts. The initiate sees here his financial fortune threatened and his business fail.

8th Hour: The Astral virtues of the elements of the seeds of every kind.

9th Hour: Nothing has ended yet. The initiate increases his vision towards the limits of the intangible world. He arrives to the infinite threshold. The divine light reveals and new dangers appear.

10th Hour: The doors of Heaven open and the man comes out of his lethargy. This is the second Initiation of the Major

Mysteries and the initiate travels in his Etheric body. It is the wisdom of John the Baptist.

11th Hour: Angels, Cherubims and Seraphims fly; there is joy in the sky. The earth awakens and the sun arises from Adam. This belongs to the great Initiations of the Major Mysteries where only the terror of the law reigns.

12th Hour: The towers of fire are disturbed. This is the triumphal entry of the Master into the happiness of Nirvana or his renunciation of it for the love of humanity, which leads him to be a Bodhisattva of compassion.

Week Eight Exercises

Astral Explorations

Introduction

From this week onwards, we are going to reinforce the techniques for Astral projection that you have learnt and in many ways, we are going to put them to the test. It will be worth your while following these Astral programs as best as you can and to do them with a serious commitment for you to have good results.

These Astral programs can show you, if you are successful, that you can investigate things in the Astral and that you can go to places and learn about them for yourself. You will also have the chance of making many attempts during this week to Astral project, and some of you may even be able to do it a few times in one single night. This will show you that the more you try, the better you get at it as you learn to eliminate the obstacles and correct your weaknesses and mistakes.

All the exercises you have done with all the techniques you have been taught will become very useful.

Journey to the Summit of Mount Everest

This first Astral exploration is to go to the summit of Mount Everest in the Astral plane. A good way to get prepared for this type of exercise is to set yourself up to do your exercises during the day and your Astral exercises at night.

I am going to outline the steps you need to follow to make sure that you successfully achieve the exercise for this week. There are a few important points you need to take into account for a successful Astral projection experience.

Daytime Exercises

Daytime exercises are very important for waking up in dreams. You can do exactly the same job in the Astral by waking up in a dream as when you have projected from your bed.

Here are the steps to follow during the day for this week:

1. Questioning - During the day, question yourself genuinely as much as you can, whether you are in the physical or in the Astral world and take a little jump or pull your finger.

2. Visualization - Visualize the summit of Mount Everest for 10 or more minutes every day. This should be done at a different time from your Astral exercise. Before visualizing it, look at a picture of the mountain and observe it in detail. Close your eyes and try to remember the details of it and recreate the image. If you have forgotten the details, open your eyes again, look at them and try to recreate them again in your mind and so on. Once you have done that, start your visualization without the picture and try to go deeper, following the second technique of visualization. You begin to go deeper into it by perceiving, visualizing the mountain tops, the snow, the sun shining, the wind, the cold, etc.

Night Time Exercises

We are going to make use of three opportunities to project for this week: when you go to bed at night, by setting your alarm and waking at 4 a.m. in the morning and when you wake up in the morning to get up for the day.

These exercises deal with the techniques you have learnt in this course so far. It is important to try your best when carrying out the exercises set for the night, making a big and sustained effort for this week not to give in to comfort and laziness.

Remember that the fear of not being able to sleep can keep you awake, or make you feel as though you are awake, when if fact you could be snoring, which is very common. Your sleep may not be a heavy one, but you will be in this amazing transition period between wakefulness and sleep; in other words, within the magical moment of Astral projection. Your aim is to create the conditions within yourself to have a conscious Astral projection, and the techniques for Astral projection do that. Make a further effort to go far enough into the exercise in order for you to be able to succeed.

Here is an outline of the steps for the night time exercises.

1. Setting Your Alarm Clock for 4 a.m. in the Morning - Setting the alarm clock at this time is a good way of achieving Astral projection or successfully waking up in your dreams.

Set your alarm clock to go off once during the night, which will be for 4 a.m. in the morning. This means you need to try to go to bed early. In order to wake yourself up a little, get up and walk around, but not too much. This is so that heavy sleep does not override you when you are going to try your Astral exercise.

Once you are doing your Astral exercise, you need to learn to not go along with thoughts that say you are awake and that you cannot sleep. You may be able to hear physical noises that tell you that you are awake. However, you may be fluctuating in the transition period between wakefulness and sleep and you think you are awake. If you are don't go along with those thoughts, which try to stop you from carrying on with the exercise, you will see that you could get the sensations and achieve a successful Astral projection or maybe even a successful waking up in your dreams.

2. Astral Projection – Start by doing the conjurations. Then begin your relaxation and ask for divine assistance in your Astral exercise. Once you are relaxed, use whichever method of Astral projection you would like to try, ranging from mantras to concentration on the heart and visualization. Perhaps you would like to try a different technique each day, or use the one you are most successful with during the whole week. However, remember that you need to plan ahead which technique you are going to use and do not change it once you have started. If you change techniques, it will throw your exercise into a mechanical mode and can ruin it. Once you have chosen the technique you are going to use, you should stick to it even if you think it is not going well. Your persistence will give you will power to succeed.

3. Travel to Mount Everest in the Astral Plane – Assuming that you have successfully Astral projected or woken up in your dreams, the next step is to go to the summit of Mount

Everest. You could ask your Divine Mother (the female aspect of your Being) to take you to the summit of Mount Everest and take a little jump. Once you are traveling, avoid being distracted by anything; otherwise, you could be back in your body almost immediately. If there are obstacles that are trying to stop you from getting to your destination, you must remain calm and relaxed, and not be confused by them, or you could visualize Mount Everest to go there.

4. Remember Your Dreams – In the morning when you wake up, use the technique to remember your dreams as you may have woken up in your dreams, but a heavy sleep may have wiped out your memory of it. You may also have actually traveled to Mount Everest without being self-aware and therefore registered it as no more than a dream. This has happened to many students, so check in your dreams this week for any information about the exercise. If you carry out your exercise for remembering dreams you may also find very useful information for your inner work in relation to your psychology, symbols and things you need to learn.

This weekly program needs to be carried out every single night for the whole week for it to have the best chance of success. You will need to be consistent with it to get into the exercise and to get better at it with each day.

Week 9

WHERE TO GO FROM HERE

*T*his is the final topic of the Astral course, but although it is the last, it is really just the beginning of the Astral exploration.

It is one thing to get into the Astral plane, but another to be an esotericist. Anyone can fly and explore the Astral world, but few penetrate its secrets.

To do that, much more information about what is there is required. You will find this on the other courses in this series – Searching Within, Journey to Enlightenment and Advanced Investigation.

Many people are no doubt content to dabble and experiment here and there, and will move on from this course to other Astral methods and courses given elsewhere. Others will want to explore deeper into the nature of themselves and life and it is these latter people that may one day be the walkers of the esoteric Path in the future.

I have given only a tiny amount of what I know about the higher and lower realms on this course. There is only so much information that can be given, practiced and understood in a nine-week course - after this there is so much more to learn. Being in the Astral plane is a way to get knowledge, but if you don't change and walk along the esoteric Path, you will never get real knowledge or wisdom. You will only get basic and usually inaccurate information and will have to muddle your way through a complex web of experiences that you have little way of understanding.

There is much more to learn and do. This course laid the foundation for the exploration of the Astral world, but future courses will give information about the bigger picture of what is there. On those courses, you will be able to practice and use what you have learnt on this one to explore and discover the nature both of yourself and of the scheme of things in life. Then you will become better equipped as an investigator and searcher into reality.

I will outline some things you can do so that you can continue your Astral exploration and practice in an effective way in the future. To begin with however, I suggest that you look back at what you have achieved in this nine-week period.

Looking Back Over This Course

By looking back over this course you may see things that worked for you and things that didn't. It's worth trying to understand why things turned out the way they did: why some exercises succeeded while others failed.

Observe what you did when successes happened, how close you came to successes and importantly, what you actually did in terms of practicing the exercises that were given on the course.

What you have achieved in this nine-week period will have been largely due to the efforts you made in it.

When looking back it is very easy to see how things could have been done better, so have a look at the mistakes you made, times when you didn't try, did something else, didn't follow the program and so on.

Resolve to correct whatever mistakes you have found if you decide to progress to the next course and keep looking for and correcting mistakes. If you do this, you will be able to make real improvements and will be able to advance in your esoteric search.

With the understanding gained by looking back over this course, you can work out your future Astral exercises and strategy, improving upon what you did before.

Bear in mind that no Astral strategy exists outside the context of daily life, and it is that which greatly affects all aspects of anyone's Astral life and experiences.

Planning the Exercises and Your Astral Strategy

Planning and organizing your time and activities is very important. If you want the Astral exercises to work, you will have to make a special effort now the Astral course is over, so it will be valuable to plan ahead and look at your whole life strategy, taking into account what importance you place on exploring the higher dimensions and getting esoteric knowledge. If you decide to do further courses in this series, you will be able to fit your Astral explorations into a wider esoteric framework. Further exercises will be given in these other courses.

When you plan what you are going to do ahead - stick to it

229

until you find something better. If you don't keep to your program, you will find that the Astral practice and experience easily falls away. It takes a lot of effort to build up and not much to lose it. Additionally, the events that take place in daily life have a way of taking your attention away from the esoteric work, so you need to be very disciplined in order to keep going and to achieve your goals in the Astral.

Using a Diary

Planning and organizing your time and activities is very important. It is an effective way to plan if you work out in a diary (it's worth getting one if you don't have one) a structure for your daily exercises.

In this way, you become organized and you know what you're going to do and whether or not you have done it.

Plan your overall strategy with all the exercises you intend to use. Then draw up a weekly schedule of exercises. In it, work out the times that you are going to spend doing the exercises and work out which ones you will do. Update the weekly schedule each week.

Each morning add any new exercises that are specific to that day if you have any, and write down each of the activities that you need to do for that day. Firstly, create a time slot for the most important ones, then for the rest.

This will allow you to do what you need to get done and will create order in daily activities, which helps towards order in thoughts. By putting in times you can also see when you have indulged in something and became lazy.

This of course doesn't stop you from taking any opportunity that you might have during the day to practice any of the exercises.

Because of entropy (as explained on this course), you may find this plan loses its effectiveness over time. Then re-appraise what you are doing and draw up your strategy again, observing what things succeeded, what failed and why. Use what you have learned to draw up a more effective strategy.

A tip for using a diary is not to be absolutely rigid with it, but to use common sense. When a more important matter arises while you are doing something, deal with it. Once it's finished go back to what you were working on. Remember that there is only so much that you can do in one day. If you work out your routine and do everything as orderly as you can, you will be able to make time, under most circumstances, for your Astral exercises.

Developing an Esoteric Framework for Daily Life

Any kind of esoteric exploration like Astral travel requires a sustained effort to succeed and to develop. However, there are many other activities in life that require our attention and it is so easy to neglect the Astral exercises particularly if there has not been any success, or if the successes happened some time ago. As soon as the interest wanes, other things seem far more important or pleasurable. Before we know it, the exercises have reduced in their frequency, or have stopped. Perhaps too, they were never even started with much dedication, as it is common to hope that success will come with as little effort as possible.

But there is no escaping the fact that a certain amount of dedicated and sustained effort has to go into achieving success in this field. So how do we do it? Besides the activity that interest itself allows, creating a lifestyle in which your esoteric development is of paramount importance, is vital.

That involves living daily life remembering your esoteric

exercises and practicing.

It is important to be aware of what you actually do throughout the day. A life lived without inner esoteric practice will be divorced from the Astral practices and the Astral explorations will be little more than a hobby.

Astral explorations need to be part of one's way of living and ones way of living must be firstly based upon esoteric work for there to be real meaning and significance to Astral travels.

The things that the mind thinks of throughout the day and the desires one has are vitally important to the actual direction that one takes in both the internal and external life. Even if someone professes to be a spiritual person for example, whether this is true or not is really in what they actually think, feel and do.

Planning and doing Astral exercises is not just a matter of creating a list of activities that are held together by a written framework based on Astral travel. Rather it is about changing the way that one thinks, feels and acts.

If you take up the courses that follow this one and develop your esoteric work seriously, you will be able to work with a clear goal and create a much more solid esoteric framework by which you live your life.

This will help you to draw up routines and to get your frame of mind directed towards your exercises. It will help you to remember to practice throughout the day; it will enable you to direct your daily activities towards esoteric work and will give you a much greater ability to succeed.

If you do decide to go further with this series of courses, I would advise that as much as possible you try to make use of every event in life to learn from yourself and to carry out the esoteric work. Learn to use each moment, and build up the esoteric work that you do so that it is the main center of your focus, drive, and interest. Live each day like this and your life will be radically transformed.

Dedication and Discipline

It is possible to have Astral experiences here and there when trying to project, but for the Astral exercises to work with any regularity one must be completely dedicated to them. To be able to project consistently requires a very strong effort throughout each day and this means being disciplined and orderly, staying focused upon the esoteric work, in whatever you are doing.

Discipline in relation to the physical body is also very important for Astral projection, since the body and the mind need to get used to a different way of approaching sleep. It takes a lot of effort and willpower, but it does pay off.

If you continue with further courses, always maintain your Astral exercises. They will be the means with which you can investigate, experience and prove what is written in them and will allow you to acquire your own esoteric knowledge - far beyond what you can read in any book. The experiences you get will always be remembered and will help you to get through the difficult times of life and the esoteric Path, building the foundation of a faith that derives from knowledge and direct experience - something that very few people have.

Overcoming Obstacles

There are many obstacles to overcome when learning about Astral projection and more again to sustain the ability. Unfortunately, most people don't work to overcome the obstacles, but those who do, find success.

This may involve sacrifices and big efforts, but rather than falling down and staying down, it's better to see what the obstacles are, to persist, and to overcome them. Then you get not only experience, but strength and willpower that will help you in many avenues of your life.

What sometimes seems like an insurmountable obstacle may be overcome with patience, effort, and further esoteric work. You need to see the particular obstacles that you face in order to overcome them. I am going to mention some of the common problems that can be overcome if you are willing to put some work into it, since in life nothing is given for free. Everything costs something and some of these costs are in effort, time, and determination. These are just a few examples; problems of all kinds arise in so many different ways again and again. It's important to keep track of your main goal and to work to overcome them, within whatever limitations you may or may not have.

Problems With Laziness

Laziness can be a very big obstacle in Astral projection. It is a problem not only for Astral projection but also for the spiritual work as a whole.

Laziness in itself is an inner state, a psychological defect. Besides doing the psychological work to reduce and remove laziness as I indicate in other courses, you also need to go against laziness by doing something even when you don't feel like doing it. If you don't do this, you will always stay trapped within those feelings that it brings. If you do the activity that laziness is trying to stop you from doing, you will gain inner strength and willpower.

Sometimes laziness is difficult to spot. It can hide itself behind very nice excuses, which can sound convincing at times and which one likes to hear and go along with, but don't be deceived by them. It's just the way that laziness operates in order to trick someone.

Many people find that at the beginning of the course laziness is not there so much in relation to the Astral exercises, because they are eager to try something new. The eagerness continues if they see things happening and working. However, when things stop happening and the morale goes down, they begin to slow down, and begin to listen to those excuses more and more. Soon laziness and entropy begin to settle. Then it's easy to forget what needs to be done for success in the Astral plane and eventually to consider giving it up.

Not only the body, but the mind is controlled by laziness, so you literally need to make yourself practice your exercises. For example, go to your room or sit down/lay down where you normally do your exercise and do it. If you have let the momentum slip and are out of practice, get back into it gradually so that you re-educate yourself. Start with an exercise for a very short period of time - up to 10 minutes, but no more. If you do it any longer when you are starting back, the difficulties that you may face can mean that you may create an additional resistance to the exercises, so get back into it gradually but methodically.

By doing this you will bring back the mode and momentum of doing the exercises. Eventually you begin to see a light at the end of the tunnel and you gradually regain the work.

Feeling Disheartened

There is a big difference between reading and talking about Astral projection, and actually doing it yourself. Sometimes expectations are different to reality and many discover that it takes a lot more work to Astral project than they had thought. Experiencing Astral travel can sound simple enough to do and yet can actually be difficult to do.

It is very easy then to become disheartened, to think that you can't do it and then to consider giving up.

But it is important to realize that it is something that has to be learned, just like any new skill. That is why you need to 'practice the exercises' because it is a process of learning. You are unlikely to Astral project as soon as you have the techniques, and even if you do, repeat success takes much work and maintaining it even more. But the exercises are given so that you learn with patience how to do them. Learning any new skill takes time and effort. A consistent daily effort and an ongoing program makes all the difference.

It's important to get into a routine and begin to build up just like is done in sports. No one becomes good at sports overnight; neither would someone who has been away from training be good at it overnight. They need to go back into it, gradually training themselves again until they reach the point where they left and improve from there. If the consistency is there, then you become good at it because you learn how it works and you gradually know the way you behave psychologically and physically when you are trying the exercises.

Problems at home, at work, or even a visit somewhere for a period of time, can sometimes throw your routine out of the window, so efforts need to be made to get back into the routine of practice again and again.

Problems With Pain and Illness When Doing Astral Exercises

Feeling pain can be enough to stop the exercise of Astral projection. Pain can commonly arise when trying to project when overdoing it, when recovering from an illness, or when you are not used to the exercises.

When the body feels pain it automatically withdraws from the cause of pain, so you will sometimes feel negative towards the exercises if you have pushed yourself or forced your body to go through pain when trying them.

Therefore, it's not advisable to push the body to the point of pain. The body and the mind must be trained gently and gradually to do the exercises. The capacity of endurance of the physical body varies from person to person. After an illness, the body is even more sensitive and vulnerable to pain and discomfort and therefore greater care should be taken. When the body has gone through an illness it will not take long to get tired or feel pain. Therefore, the best thing is to try the exercises for very short periods of time, according to what the body can tolerate, before it becomes painful or uncomfortable.

After illness it would be best to start with very short relaxation exercises. Then if you are able, increase the time each day until you feel ready to practice Astral projection, but never force the body. See what you can take and don't push it; build up gradually.

If you are simply trying to go back into the exercises because you have drifted away from them and you feel pain when you do the exercises, the approach is similar. However, it will take less time to get back into the exercises since the body only has to be trained to remain still in a position for a while. At the same time, the mind will need to go back to the discipline of focusing on the exercises.

The main thing in both cases is to get started in the exercises,

237

gradually going further each time. If you persist, you will eventually wake up in your dreams and/or experience Astral projection. Once that happens, carry on with your daily exercises, maintaining and increasing them.

Like most things, these exercises improve with practice, so it's important to be continuous and consistent with them. This also implies patience and lots of it is needed, since we have to re-educate ourselves out of old patterns of behavior into new ones. This takes time and effort to do. When the continuity in the exercises is lost, for whatever reason, it needs to be built back up again.

You also have to watch that you don't force yourself. Increase the time spent practicing gradually, so that you get used to it. Stop if you feel you are forcing something or if the body rebels and feels uncomfortable with it.

Entropy

There is another factor in bringing down the momentum of any activity including the Astral exercises: that is entropy. A new activity starts on a high note generally and progresses up to a certain point. After that point, things begin to slide back downwards until they reach the starting point. If the same or less effort is made through the life of an activity, it will inevitably slide back down due to the forces of nature. The way out of this is to apply an additional factor, usually an effort that brings the activity up in its notes and, like a musical scale, it can continue rising in higher octaves until another effort is needed and so on. This counters the force of the entropy; if that extra effort is not made things will go back to their starting point.

Therefore, when something interesting and new starts there is an eagerness to try it and so generally good efforts are made.

The eagerness continues if you see things happening and working. However, if things stay the same and additional effort is not made, then inevitably things stop happening and the note goes down. It will fall back unless you review what you are doing and provide an extra 'shock' with extra work - do that and you keep progressing. This applies to any activity.

Getting into a Mode of Practicing

When applying extra effort or to begin making efforts again, you should aim to get into the mode of practicing. This is the feeling of when things are flowing well, and often requires considerable effort to achieve.

When you get caught up in the fascination with daily activities, with a job, with friends, with the family and so on, the esoteric work slips away and its importance is easily forgotten or pushed to one side, but that doesn't mean that it actually has lost its importance - it's just that you can't see it any more. It is far more important than you can imagine and when this life is over it is all that really matters. Time that is wasted is never recovered again.

The Ability to Concentrate

Concentrating upon the exercise you are doing is a vital part of the routine for Astral projection, and any routine that you have must include working towards developing this ability to be successful consistently. If you don't do it, the mind will never be properly trained or educated to be on the exercise you are doing, and then even the best techniques of projection are not very effective.

When you do your exercise to project and the mind keeps thinking about other things, it's due to a lack of practice in being focused during the day and indicates the need for extra or for more or consistent daily practice.

The concentration and visualization exercises can be incorporated into your daily routine fairly easily, but it takes a great deal of willpower to be aware of what you are doing throughout the day.

Being Concentrated Upon What You Are Doing During the Day

If you can get used to being focused and concentrated upon what you are doing, then when you go to Astral project, you're used to being on one thing and the mind has much less activity, because when we are on one thing, the mind gets quietened, instead of being scattered in all kinds of different activities. When the mind is scattered like that, you tend think about lots of different things at one time and the mind goes on compulsively in a scattered, disordered way.

So if you do one thing at a time and, if possible finish it, or finish what you need to do on it before moving on to the next thing, you will create much more order and usually efficiency in your daily activities.

This also has an effect upon the quality and type of dreams at night. The important thing is to concentrate upon whatever activity you are doing at the time and to do only one activity at a time. Even if you have a lot of tasks to do and are under pressure, deal with the most important one, giving it your full attention, even if it is just for a few moments before you have to do another task. Give whatever you are doing at that moment your full attention.

Further Courses

There are three more courses in this series if you want to explore what you have learnt on this course further.

The Searching Within course explains about psychology, about self-knowledge and how to acquire it. The Journey to Enlightenment course explains about the overall picture of life and death and how to convert oneself into a spiritual Being. The Advanced Investigation course gives the opportunity to concentrate upon the exercises in an intensive way.

Finally, I will add that it is much easier to succeed in Astral travel if you can study with other people, rather than studying in isolation. There are study centers that teach these courses for free in different locations around the world. By studying at one of these, you can also get to meet like-minded people and be part of an environment that is good for inner exploration and development.

If you want more information on these courses and study centers go to the Gnosticweb website www.gnosticweb.com

Week Nine Exercises

A Group Astral Exercise

A Group Exercise to Meet Together in One Place in the Astral Plane

In this last week of the course, all the students from all over the world join in one group, in an effort to meet their fellow-students in the Astral at some of the major sites throughout the world.

Although the book of this course only gives the one example of a place to travel to, the meeting place is changed with each new course online and in the study centers.

As well as getting the opportunity of getting esoteric knowledge, this exercise will give you the opportunity to experience what it takes to make such a journey and also to see that it is actually possible to meet other people in the Astral plane. Make all the efforts you can to follow the schedule of exercises for this Astral program. It could be that you will make it if you dedicate this week to this exercise.

Participating in this exercise is a very good opportunity. Just like last week, practice your exercises during the day and also the exercises for the night. Don't be too concerned whether you are within the right time frame to meet other students. Since time is different in the Astral plane and as this exercise involves every student of the world, you will find that someone somewhere will be trying to Astral project at around the same time as you, so it's just a matter of making sure that you do your part in getting there.

Meeting at the Great Pyramids of Egypt

This final week's exercise is to try to go to the Pyramids of Egypt. Everyone on the course can try to go there to see what is really there in the Astral, perhaps to discover some hidden mystery, or to learn about their origin or functions. Perhaps to meet with other students on the course, or to receive true esoteric teachings. Pyramids are places of ascension. In their higher spiritual aspect they symbolize the three mountains of the esoteric Path and in astronomical terms the three Great Pyramids correspond to Orion's belt.

To get there, practice the Astral this week with this goal in mind. You can use mantras or visualization for it.

If you use mantras for this exercise, use the Egyptian ones: Egypto or Fa Ra On.

Before you start, visualize the Pyramids - visualize yourself actually being there in person. Then, once you perceive them clearly, begin your visualization or mantra.

If you use a mantra for this particular exercise on the Pyramids, pronounce it around seven times aloud and stay with the image of the Pyramid without exploring it further. Then pronounce the mantra mentally while continuing to hold the image for the duration of the exercise.

If you use visualization alone to try to project, imagine that you are visiting a Pyramid as you go to sleep. Vividly and realistically explore it with your imagination. Visualize yourself there - go inside, walk or travel through it and explore it. Do this as you are going to sleep, maintaining it as sleep arrives.

You may go directly to the Pyramids when you project, or go there in a dream state and dream about it. If you Astral project into your room or some other place, ask your Divine Mother to take you to the Pyramids and visualize them so that you go there.

Before doing any of these Astral exercises, ask your Being for help in projecting and assistance to get to the Pyramids. If you get there, look carefully at what you see. If you see someone there, ask them if they are a Gnostic. They may be a student from the course, or maybe even a true Gnostic, that is an Initiate or a Master of the White Lodge. If you intuitively sense that something is wrong or that someone you see there is not right, don't forget to use the conjurations.

Try this exercise for the whole of this week.

Here are the steps for the exercise in more detail:

1. Familiarize Yourself With the Place – Have a look at pictures of the Great Pyramids of Egypt and familiarize yourself with the place. In your visualization exercises, use your senses so that you can visualize the place in as much detail as you can. Visualize the real size of the Pyramids, the stones that they have been made of, the smell of the surroundings, the sun shining and whatever else you want to investigate about them.

2. Use Your Astral Projection Techniques – Use the techniques of concentration/visualization and/or mantras you have learnt on the course to project there.

3. Waking Up in the Astral from a Dream – Throughout the week question yourself whether you are in the physical or in the Astral with the real doubt that you could be dreaming. For example, are you sure that you are reading this Astral program in the physical? Are you sure? Have you pulled your finger or jumped to find out? If you haven't yet, you should do it now, because you could be in the Astral world.

This kind of questioning is a back up exercise. This means that if you have not consciously Astral projected from your bed, you still have the chance to travel to the Great Pyramids of Egypt, if you wake up in your dreams. Therefore, take every opportunity you can. Every time you remember, question yourself whether you really are in the physical or in the Astral, and work towards making this technique your springboard to get you to your destination. You should also remember that you need to try to be as aware as much as you can in the physical world so that you are more aware in the Astral.

4. The Exercise Timetable During Weekdays – The exercise to meet in one place needs to be carried out every night during this week as you are going to sleep. Choose the Astral technique that suits you best. Use last week's timetable of waking up just once in the night at 4am as well for this week, but don't use the intensive Saturday night timetable that follows, as that will be too tiring to maintain all week.

5. Saturday Night Astral Exercise – For this week on Saturday night only, people attend the study centers for a series of Astral exercises, with the goal of going to the meeting place in the Astral plane. So if you can, set aside Saturday night to follow this same program.

Here is the schedule of Saturday Astral projection times and techniques to follow:

10 p.m. - Concentration/visualization on the Great Pyramids of Egypt.

12 a.m. - Pronounce the mantra Fa Ra On and visualize the Pyramids.

2 a.m. - Pronounce the mantra Egypto and visualize the Pyramids.

4 a.m. - Pronounce the mantra Fa Ra On and visualize the Pyramids.

6. Setting Your Alarm Clock for Saturday Night – On Saturday set the alarm clock to go off at the above times. They start at 10 p.m. and finish at 8 a.m. the next morning. If you do this program, try to go to bed early if possible, so that you are not tired the next day. When you wake up during the night, try to wake yourself up a little in order to be able to have a go at your Astral exercise. This can be difficult, but an extra effort sometimes has to be made so that heavy sleep does not override you when you try your exercises.

7. Conjure and Ask for Spiritual Help in the Exercise – Before you start your Astral projection exercise, don't forget to conjure and begin your relaxation exercise. It is also very important to ask for divine assistance in this exercise so that you have the strength to do it and also the guidance and the protection you need to do it well.

8. What to Do When You Get Into the Astral – Like last week, ask your Divine Mother (the female aspect of your Being) to take you to the Great Pyramids of Egypt and travel there, or visualize them and go straight there.

9. What to Do Once You Are at the Meeting Place in the Astral Plane – Once you are at the Pyramids you will get what is due for you. However, one experiment you could do is to ask whether there is anyone there from this course. If anyone approaches you, ask him/her whether he or she is a student from these courses and ask their name. You may be surprised to find that one of your fellow students may have that name, and both of you may be able to confirm in the physical plane that you have met in the Astral as some students have already done with this exercise. If you do meet someone who says they are from the courses, unless you know them personally you should post an account of your meeting in the online forums to check whether anyone can account for the meeting too, or whether someone has already posted something about meeting you. Don't forget however that you should always use your intuition and be open to receiving teachings. Things may not always happen as you expect in the Astral plane and you shouldn't allow preconceptions from the physical world to interfere there.

10. Remember Your Dreams – In the morning when you wake up, use the technique to remember your dreams as you may have woken up in your dreams, but the heavy sleep may have wiped out your memory of it. Or you may have actually traveled to the meeting place without being self-aware and therefore registered it as no more than a dream. This has happened to many students, so check in your dreams this week for any information about the exercise. If you remember dreams you may also find very useful information for your inner work in relation to your psychology, symbols and things you need to learn.

Daily feedback for this exercise can be posted in the specific forum allocated for this Group Astral Exercise in the online course.

* * *

Now that it is the end of the course, I am going to mention a technique of Astral projection that didn't make it into the course. I'll give some questions and answers and students results of this weeks group Astral projection exercise and will list the exercises that have been used on the course.

An Extra Exercise of Astral Projection: Watching the Dream Images

This exercise is a little hit and miss compared with the exercises that have been given on the course. It is so easy just to fall asleep and not to develop any particular skill such as concentration or pronouncing mantra, so try this exercise if you wish in the future. I have used it successfully, but you really do have to get the timing right.

To do the exercise, relax the body as normal lying on your back if you're comfortable like that. Then keep relaxing into the sleep. Watch for the first dream images and then get up slowly from bed. If you catch it at the right moment, you will get up in the Astral.

You have to watch that you don't miss the opportunity and fall asleep instead; it takes a bit of practice. These dream images are different from thoughts. They appear to be almost real and you will know them when you experienced them, if you haven't done so already.

There is a variation on this exercise, which is to go back into a dream. If you remember the dream when you wake up, you can go back into it. This is useful if you want to get more information on something. You just remember the dream and place yourself in it using your imagination. If you really place yourself in it and sleep arrives, you will find yourself back in that dream.

Questions and Answers

Below are a couple of questions and answers that students have had about this week's group exercise.

Q. I wonder, is there a connection between the three Pyramids at Giza and the three mountains? Also, the Pyramids had golden tops. I wonder if there is a connection there with something to do with the crown Chakra?

A. Yes, the three Pyramids do have a relation to the three mountains. The Pyramids are places of ascension; the gold tops represent the triumph, the gold of the spirit. The Egyptians had a great esoteric knowledge.

In many dreams I become lucid and can make sentient decisions i.e. I want to go to Egypt. It's just that at that point things often get messy and I wake up. I'm not sure why, but when I become lucid and decide just to watch the dream and interact minimally, the dream never lasts as long as I would like. How can I extend these experiences and gain more control?

The problem is your idea of interacting minimally. You need to act more intuitively and in a more normal way there. When

249

you get caught up in thoughts it can become messy in the Astral world.

Students' Experiences of the Group Astral Exercises

Below is a small selection of experiences that students have had with this week's group exercise. The names have been removed or changed.

The homework for the week was to practice the Astral intensively all week and to go to the Pyramids of Egypt to meet with other students as well as to see how they look in the Astral Plane. We were to use Egyptian mantras like 'Egypto', 'Fa Ra On' and 'La Ra S', or a visualization exercise on the Pyramids.

I practiced hard all week with a strong determination at the study center, with other students and at home. At the end of the week, all students of the study centers decided to do a night practice. We all agreed to come to our centers at 3 a.m. and try the practice until 5 a.m. and that is when I had my little success with the homework given.

We all chanted the mantra 'La Ra S' aloud seven times and then internally, feeling the vibrations of the mantra throughout the body and, at the same time, keeping a still image of the Pyramids. I started the mantra, but fell into a light sleep. Then I woke up and continued the mantra and as sleep started to arrive again, I made an extra effort to concentrate on the mantra. Soon after, I started to feel my body temperature rising and the whole body vibrating and intuition told me that it was time to get up. However, I hesitated to do so as it felt so much like the physical that I thought that if I move I would wake up the others, but intuition was telling me, "Get up, you are in the Astral!" so I did.

I rolled over to the side and got up from the floor as I would do in the physical. I found it very hard to move and I couldn't open my eyes, so I sang the mantra Bellilin and the darkness went away. I looked around the practice room and saw the Astral body of one of the students. Her Astral body was unconscious, sitting down playing with her hands. I went outside the room by going through the door. I walked around the center and saw how it looks in the Astral.

I went down the stairs trying to stay in the moment so that nothing such as an emotion or a thought could throw me back to my body. I went through the door of the room downstairs where more students were practicing and saw the room full of people - more than the ones who were practicing. I saw the Astral bodies of many people - sitting cross-legged, walking around looking at the room, talking to each other... These could have been the Astral bodies of people that come to the study center or of people that will come to the center in the near future.

However, I didn't want to get distracted by talking to them; I had to go to the Pyramids! I went outside the center and took a few minutes to ask my Divine Mother with all my heart and strength to take me to the Pyramids of Egypt so that I experience and learn. Then I did a small vertical jump thinking that she would guide me on my flight there, but to my surprise she took me towards the ground and I made my journey to Egypt going through the planet. I couldn't see anything, nor did I feel that I was going through a hard surface. She simply took me the quickest and easiest way so I wouldn't get distracted on the way. I landed in a room surrounded by big glass windows. From there I could see the three Pyramids from far away and just with the thought of wanting to get closer, I did. There were a lot of people around the place doing various things, some conscious and some unconscious. I gather that many spiritual groups focus on the Pyramids and that many others dream about the Pyramids so their Astral body goes there even if unconscious. I could also have seen personalities of people that have passed away.

I saw the Pyramids in two ways, but I can't give too much detail

251

because of the esoteric or internal nature of the information. I walked amongst the multitude and called out aloud, "Are there any students of Gnosis around?" I caught the attention of several people and two of them came closer to shake my hand, but my intuition told me to be precocious with them. I ignored them and kept walking and observing. Then I decided to invoke a Master and as I was calling, I went back to my physical body due to a big emotion.

From this experience I not only learnt aspects about my internal work but also the reality of the Divine Mother. She guides us and shows us what we need to see. She doesn't leave our side but yet we can't see her because she is so incredibly divine that her light and presence would blind us.

I also learnt that determination and faith makes a big difference when trying to do a practice.

Hilda

Yes, and also the preparation that you did for a week beforehand, the effort made to go to the study center and the esoteric strength generated by the group practice.

The Pyramids of Egypt

In the study center, we had a night of Astral practices with a group of students to try and project to the Pyramids of Egypt. We did a variety of practices throughout the night, but the one I was most enthusiastic about was the visualization of the Pyramids. I imagined myself actually being there, walking around the outside of the Pyramids, exploring inside, and even standing at the peak looking out over Egypt. After a while my physical body began falling asleep and I felt myself lift out of my body into the Astral.

I was in the practice room of the study center. I asked for divine help to be taken to the Pyramids and straight away I felt myself turn over so I was looking face down at the floor and I was being pulled downwards. I knew I was being taken to the Pyramids, but in the Astral I had only ever flown somewhere or found myself in a place straight away. I had never gone down through the earth and I felt apprehensive. I was soon back in my body. I kept concentrating and again I lifted out of my body and asked to be taken to the Pyramids. The same thing occurred. I was being pulled to the floor, but could not go through it even though I wanted to. Back and forth I went from the physical to the Astral about seven times, each time being pulled towards the floor once I was in the Astral. On the last occasion, I was hovering, nose to the carpet in the Astral and I looked to the side and saw that the student that was next to me in the practice room was in her Astral body. She looked at me surprised and asked me what I was doing. I told her that I was trying to get through the floor to go to the Pyramids, but couldn't because I was a bit fearful. She looked amused. At that point, I seemed to black out and suddenly found myself flying at high speed over a beautiful place. There was an amazing building below and I flew down to it. I spent a short time there, but to this day I am still not sure if that place was linked to the Pyramids or not. The next morning we shared our experiences, and the student who had been next to me, remembered seeing me in the Astral and vaguely recalled the conversation. It had been an extraordinary night.

Debbie

The Great Pyramid Khufu

In order to prepare the practice I tried to get most of the information about the Great Pyramids. I found the position of the Pyramids next to the Sphinx, the entrances, the passages - all the information. I was shocked because during the Sphinx projection practice I had walked around the Pyramids, so I was a little familiar with them. In any case, I managed to project Saturday 9 a.m. (GMT-Universal Time).

I created the circle of protection and projected using mantra Egypto and visualization. I projected to the Sphinx as before, and from there, I continued to the Pyramids, investigated inside (Khufu and Menkaure), etc. At the door I waited asking for anyone from the course, but I did not feel anybody.

Last night, back at home, I projected at 4:10 a.m. Monday GMT. I followed the same procedure. This time I projected directly to the door of the Great Pyramid of Khufu. Just when I arrived, I began asking for anyone from the course. At the beginning I saw a couple of masks, and immediately conjured Bellilin. I continued and next thing I saw a middle-aged female face, with blonde hair and thick-white glasses. I asked if she was from the course, but I got no response. I continued asking for people from the course. I felt a couple hand-in-hand going by, but nobody said anything. I came back at 4:45 a.m.

Gareth

The Journey to Bethlehem

The practice was to get to Bethlehem and invoke the Master Jeshua Ben Pandira on Christmas Eve, waking at intervals throughout the night to do so. It was an unofficial practice organized by one of the trainee teachers over the Christmas break.

Having felt the weight of lost opportunities before, I didn't want to pass up this one, knowing the strength that everyone online practicing would create. So even though I knew the next day would be long with relatives and so forth, in this practice I gave it a good go, getting up at every alarm and going into each practice with determination.

Throughout the week I had also really investigated what it is to check what dimension you are in. For a long time I haven't actually understood how to do this, so lately I have really been looking at pulling my finger consciously rather than mentally. I find the all night practices really give me something to work towards, an immediate goal, just like a race that an athlete works towards.

I visualized Bethlehem in detail, imagining myself walking down a rocky pathway into the city, the buildings of which were silhouetted against the luminescent starry night sky. Above me was a particularly bright star, leading me to the birthplace of Jesus Christ. I could feel the warm desert wind and hear the silence of the desert night (and even smell the donkeys!).

However, even though I didn't project from the practice, I did wake up in dreams. The first time I did, it just all of a sudden became clear and I pulled out of the subconscious automatically, then asking to be taken to Bethlehem using the conjurations to clear things as I went, finding myself in a location there. However, moments after I arrived, I fell into a dream within which I received a marvelous teaching on my approach to Astral practices, which has proved invaluable to me.

The second time I woke was as a direct result from questioning. I was walking my dog as I usually do in the afternoon, but we were a long way from our usual route. I questioned this, looking intensely at my surroundings and then became lucid as I remembered my mission to invoke the Master Jeshua Ben Pandira.

This experience demonstrated to me the results one can achieve when we create our own discipline and stick to it, seizing the opportunities that exist from moment to moment.

Jill

Mount Everest

I woke in the night last and concentrated as I went to sleep. Soon after I realized I was out of my body. I decided I should try to go to Mount Everest and I visualized being at the place in the picture. In visualizing, I didn't just picture the place, but tried to really 'feel' myself there, as I feel myself in a place when I have the awareness working right. Instantly I was there; it was as if I had 'dissolved' into this place like when a movie fades from one location to another. I

255

looked around a little and I think I recall seeing some orange colored rock cliffs around.

To be honest, I didn't take that great of a look around. Soon though, I met with a young woman. I asked her name and she said her name was 'Sal'. I believe we shook hands. She had sandy blonde hair that was pulled back. She asked me my name and I told her. I was trying hard to stay focused and not let thoughts interfere with anything. I think I took a little look around, but then I suddenly felt that she had disappeared. Then the whole thing shifted into a long lucid dream where I knew I was dreaming, but I think most of it was just subconscious projections.

Later, I spoke to a student living in Japan, posting as 'Sally', but who usually went by the name 'Sal' she said. She was the only other person who reported getting to Everest that night, and her story matched very closely to mine, though she did not actually remember seeing me. She said that she had gotten there and thought she remembered seeing people, but drifted into being not so clear, and then was woken up by her doorbell. Strange, I thought, since I recalled her suddenly and unexpectedly vanishing after we had spoken.

Bill

Below is the conversation from the online forums:

"Has anyone else been successful in going to Mount Everest for the group exercise? I became lucid in my dream this morning and began my Astral journey to Mount Everest. It was so unbelievable! Just the feeling of flying so high, so high that I was in the clouds. It was almost dawn and it was beautiful. When I started out, I couldn't see well, so I tried using the Bellilin conjuration. It worked perfectly. I could see like never before - wow! I asked the Divine Mother to help me go to my destination and I immediately found myself floating in mid air somewhere in the US (I currently live in Japan). It was great. It took some getting used to trying to maneuver around, but it got

*easier. I was almost there! I could see it. I thought that there were
other people there as well. I could feel cool air, but the doorbell rang
and brought me back! Maybe next time."*

Sally

*"I was successful at getting to Mount Everest on the same night
and I talked to someone who said her name was 'Sal' and had sandy
blonde hair pulled back. Could this be you?"*

Bill

*"I do usually call myself 'Sal', but I have reddish brown hair. I
know that I made it there that night, but I can't remember talking to
anyone. I saw that people were there, but it gets fuzzy after that and
then I woke up, so I don't know. But the whole experience was just
amazing!"*

Sally

A Visit to the Planet Mars

*I had been trying to get to the planet Mars and call the Master
Samael for a long time. I had many thwarted and even agonizing
attempts, but finally after much longing, practicing and working, it
happened.*

*The study center held their first all night practice, which was to
project to the Solar System, and then more specifically, to the planet
Mars. That night there was a lot of group strength and I managed to
get to the Solar System, but got lost in darkness and a dream.*

*The next night, inspired by the enthusiasm and magic of our first
all night practice, I woke myself at three in the morning to do an
Astral practice. I felt the sensations, but just couldn't push through
the dreamy thoughts into conscious sleep, and so rolled over.*

*I then found myself in a dream and pulled away from it, becoming
lucid, then floating happily and naturally into the sky with the ease*

257

and carefree nature of a child. I wondered for a few moments, where it was that I would like to go. Instantly I thought of the Pyramids, and asked to go there, but felt no pull towards them, instead feeling myself rising higher and higher into the sky. Seeing as I was heading into the stars, I asked my Divine Mother and Father to take me to the Solar System.

I felt a rush and found myself hovering in space, looking back through the different colored planets of the Solar System, towards the sun. A female voice then prompted me, saying that I could go to Mars if I concentrated upon it. This I did, and then watched as the planet Mars appear below me, shining in the light of the sun. I then made a determined effort to fly right into its center.

I flew with great speed towards the planet, then entering its strange atmosphere, which consisted of what seemed like huge different sized red bubbles whose surfaces were colored like oil on water, glistening with rainbow hues. There were hundreds and hundreds of them. I then began invoking the Master Samael as I moved further and further into the planet's heart, then passing through a hazy red liquid as the bubbles condensed and became smaller. At times my awareness would begin to lapse and I felt myself lose consciousness, being plunged into darkness, but each time I brought myself back, trying to remain aware as possible and not get fascinated with what I was seeing, using the call for Master Samael to center me.

It was not long then, before I found myself before the Master Samael...

Eventually my lack of awareness got the better of me, and I was pulled back to my body, then waking up, hardly able to believe where I had just been. One moment I had been in the planet Mars talking with Master Samael, and the next I was lying on my bed, in the quiet normality of my room.

Just before I left, I spoke with Master Samael, saying how hard it would be to put such an incredible experience into words. Nothing I write could do justice to such a special experience. After practicing

Astral Projection for over a year, I had not comprehended even the beginnings of what we could all be capable of, until that day.

Beryl

To the Edge of the Galaxy

When I began to take the Astral course and began to practice the techniques for Astral travel, I soon started to get results. Although I had had some success, the Astral experiences up to now had been brief. I really didn't have any idea that the Astral experience could be such a magnificent thing.

I retired for bed fairly early that night. I had experienced a really good day and had a very positive attitude towards reaching the Astral. After a brief relaxation, I began the concentration exercise. Within just a couple of minutes, I began to feel small waves of vibration in my body. The vibrations continued to get stronger until my whole body felt like a huge electric current was surging through it. The vibrations were incredibly fast as well. The next thing I knew, I was above the Earth in the vacuum of space.

After looking around briefly, I began to be drawn in one direction. I came in contact with a small odd shaped planetary body and descended closer to examine it. The color and detail of it were crystal clear. As I departed, I began to travel faster and faster. I was soon traveling at an incredible speed where stars would zoom by me. Within just a brief moment, I was hovering at the edge of the galaxy itself. I could see other spiral galaxies in the distance, and the colors were more beautiful than any I had ever seen. I was allowed to pause there for a brief time to marvel at the beauty of creation. After this, the divine Being who had brought me there took me down to another planetary body to give me an esoteric teaching, which I cannot speak of. After this, I was drawn back into my body within an instant. I sat up in bed and became almost overwhelmed with joy at such a profound experience. I will never forget it.

259

I got up and made some notes and drew some pictures of some of the things I had seen, especially the odd shaped rock in space. Three days later, I was at work and listening to the news on the radio. The next item in the news was that astronomers had just discovered a potato-shaped asteroid in the outer reaches of our Solar System. I smiled and thought, "Wow, what a way to get confirmation that it really did happen."

Salim

An Attempt to Get to Mars

My Astral experience occurred during the last practice of the night at 4 a.m. where we used the mantra Hare Ram.

I made an extra effort to fight for concentration in this practice as I had fallen asleep too quickly for the last three practices that night. During this practice I also fell asleep before consciously projecting, but woke up in a dream that was full of esoteric symbolism.

Upon becoming conscious in the Astral, I was aware that I was in the practice room at the study center. I could see everyone in the room. I remembered the goal of the night and asked for help to be taken there.

I then glided over to the window in order to fly out. At the window I was met by the Astral body of another student doing the practice. I was asked by this student for help to project into the Astral. I tried to help by extending my arm for them to grab on to, but they did not take it. I didn't wish to linger so close to my physical body for too long in case I snapped back and so I asked for help again to be taken to the planet Mars by the quickest route.

Instantly I flew out the window and made it into the Solar System. I could see the stars and feel the freedom of being in the Astral. Unfortunately, at that point I began to feel overwhelming guilt for not helping the other students to project and so quickly snapped back into my body. I tried to project again that night but could not.

It was a good experience as it gave me further insight into what I need to improve and insight into what is going on within. It also gave me determination to actually improve on those faults.

Roger

The Planet Mars

In the study center we did a group practice with the goal of projecting to the planet Mars. We chose this practice because at the time, Mars was particularly close to earth and could be seen clearly in the night sky. The idea of being able to visit it was awe-inspiring.

One of the practices we did to reach this goal was to visualize the planet and stay focused on it. I began by visualizing myself flying away from the earth and into the Solar System until I saw a glowing red planet in front of me. I imagined myself flying closer towards it until I passed through the clouds surrounding it. I looked below and imagined the giant craters, the deep canyons, and the towering mountains. I imagined walking on the surface, over the rocks and pebbles, and feeling the red dust filter between my fingers. The visualization was so enjoyable that staying focused on it was not too difficult.

As I continued with the visualization, my physical body started to fall asleep and I felt myself lift out of it and into the Astral. I flew towards the door of the practice room, stepped outside, and asked for divine help to be taken to the planet Mars, but due to a distraction I quickly returned to my physical body. I resumed the visualization of Mars and after a short period of time, I lifted out of my physical body again. This time I felt a strong pull drawing me to the other end of the practice room towards the window. I flew through it, feeling a strange sensation in my Astral body as I passed through the glass pane. I found myself standing on the road outside the study center. I looked up at the stars, amazed at their beauty, and asked for help to be taken to Mars. I took a big jump and felt myself moving at high speed into the Solar System. The experience was so overwhelming that I returned to my physical body with a jolt. I woke up remembering the experience clearly and wanting to get straight back in there to feel again the magic of the Astral.

Maria

A List of the Exercises on the Course

Finally, here is a list the various techniques that have been used on this course so that you have a record of them all together in one place.

1. Relaxation
2. Remembering dreams
3. Surface concentration
4. Imaginative concentration
5. Concentration on the heart
6. Projecting/traveling to a place
7. Waking up in dreams
8. Mantras
9. The Conjurations and the Circle of Protection
10. Awareness/concentration on activities
11. Watching the dream images (an extra exercise)

* * *

APPENDIX

Web Resources

Here is a list of Internet links to supplement the course.

Course Sign Up Page
This is the link to sign up for this course online and to have access to questions and answers in the online course forums:

http://www.gnosticweb.com/netclasses/

Study Centres Main Page
For more information about attending one of the free courses at the study centres go to:

http://www.gnosticweb.com/centres/

Sound Files
For all the sound files associated with mantras and conjurations on this course, download the mp3 files at:

http://www.gnosticweb.com/astralbook/

Gnosticweb Home Page
The home page of the main Gnosticweb site where you will find public chatrooms and forums can be found at:

http://www.gnosticweb.com

Astralweb Home Page

The website dedicated to Astral projection only is located at:

http://www.astralweb.org

Mysticweb Home Page

The website dedicated to articles and student experiences on different subjects can be found at:

http://www.mysticweb.org

Book Order Information

http://www.absolutepublishinggroup.com

INDEX

surface concentration, 50
visualization, 50
waking up in dreams, 136
watching dreams, 248
Experiences. *See* Students' experiences

F
Faculties
of intuition, 188
psychic, 31, 99, 140
Falling asleep, problems with, 64
Fantasy, 45, 110
Father, 164, 169, 190, 203, 208
Fear, 15, 201
Flying, 35, 59, 110, 203

G
Galaxy, 259
Gnostic, 6, 190, 244
Gurdjeff, 95

H
Heart, concentrating on, 57, 78-92
Hell, 12, 204
Hours, meaning of, 219

I
Illness, 199, 203, 204, 207, 212
problems with, 236
Imaginative concentration, 52
Incubus, 172
Interpreting dreams, 187-221
Intuition, 188

J
Jesus, 170, 182, 255
Journey to Enlightenment course, 5, 10, 12, 14, 16
Jupiter, 164, 173

K
Karma, 133, 199, 202, 205, 206, 208
Kundalini, 106, 133, 161, 200, 202, 210, 211

―――――――

List of Photographs:

p.163 - *The Nightmare,* 1781
Henry Fuseli
Founders Society Purchase with funds from Mr. and Mrs. Bert
L. Smokler and Mr. and Mrs. Lawrence A. Fleischman
Photograph © 1954 The Detroit Institute of Arts.

p.168 - Illustration from *The Astrologer of the Nineteenth Century*
Smith, Robert Cross (Raphael), 1825. London, England
Photograph courtesy of Thomas Sandberg, Sweden.

ABSOLUTE PUBLISHING GROUP LLC

P.O Box 99167
Emeryville, CA 94662-9167, USA
Phone: 510.938.0877
Email: info@absolutepublishinggroup.com

www.absolutepublishinggroup.com

**Distributed in USA and Canada by
Biblio Distribution, a division of National Book
Network (NBN)**

Phone (toll free ordering): 1.800.462.6420
FAX (toll free ordering): 1.800.338.4550
Email: custserv@nbnbooks.com

www.bibliodistribution.com